THE
GREAT
CHALLENGE

Lea,

Praying Hebrews 6:11
over you!

THE
GREAT
CHALLENGE
Living a Love That Reconciles

RYAN NUNEZ

New City Press

Published by New City Press
202 Comforter Blvd.,
Hyde Park, NY 12538
www.newcitypress.com

Cover design and layout by Miguel Tejerina

Library of Congress Control Number: 2020931343

ISBN: 978-1-56548-015-5 (paperback)
ISBN: 978-1-56548-020-9 (e-book)

Printed in the United States of America

Contents

Introduction

One of the things that unites all human beings is our need and desire for authentic relationship. The specific number of relationships one desires is a factor of one's personality. For some people crowds wear them out. After being in a group of people for a given length of time, their energy is depleted and can only be recharged by being away from others for a time. And then there are some people whose energy increases with every person who walks into the room.

But regardless of personality type, everyone has a fundamental need to be in relationships with others.

Of course, this is easier said than done. Relationships are hard. Actually, let me say that a different way: authentic relationships are hard. An authentic relationship takes a lot of work. It means being genuine and vulnerable, which builds trust over time. Authentic relationships require a lot of maintenance. Conflicts and disagreements need to be addressed and worked through. There are misunderstandings and sometimes there is outright betrayal.

Sometimes our relationships become so damaged we are tempted to just toss them out instead of fixing them. In some instances we are hurt so badly we believe that life would be easier without other people—that is, until it happens and we find ourselves alone. At first it might feel like carefree living. There is relief in not worrying about someone else all the time, but then the isolation sets in. When we do not have authentic relationships, the loneliness that can come even in a crowded room is unbearable.

This is not a modern phenomenon. This is a universal human condition. Across cultures and times, the need to be connected with others is ever present.

The Bible opens with an account of the first man, named Adam. God creates him and places him in a beautiful garden. He is shown love by God and given a purpose in life: he is to tend the garden and care for the creation God has placed around him. Within a very short period of time a phrase in the narrative sticks out like a sore thumb: "it is not good." The reason this is so out of place is that the introduction to this narrative about Adam is an ancient Hebrew poem describing God's creative acts. Ancient Hebrew poetry has a rhythm set out by repeating phrases. (This is different than our modern poetry or songs, whose rhythm is typically established by words that rhyme.) The repeating phrase of the poem is, "it was good." So, after hearing over and over again that everything is good, we get a "not good." And this "not good" statement happens sooner than you might think. If you have heard the account from Genesis, you know about the serpent and the forbidden fruit, the fall of mankind. But this "not good" is even before that. Do you know what is "not good"?

"It is not good for the man to be alone. I will make a helper who is just right for him" (Genesis 2:18).

We were literally created to be in relationship with others.

That's why it pains us so much to be alone.

That's why it hurts so much when relationships struggle.

William Shakespeare captures this sentiment in his play *Julius Caesar*. As Caesar is being assassinated by a group of senators, Shakespeare places in his mouth the famous line: "Et tu, Brute!" Meaning, "And you, Brutus!" He is literally being murdered, but the most traumatic part of his death is the discovery that his friend Brutus conspired against him.

We are really good at sabotaging the life-giving relationships we need. We do it through feelings of privilege, selfishness, bias, fear, and anger, to name a few. When these things find their way into our relationships the natural consequence is division.

How do we find and maintain the authentic relationships we both desire and need? The answer is not new. In fact, it is ancient. As much as we feel like the human experience has changed over time, at its core it's still the same: the same challenges, just in different packaging, the same needs, just expressed differently. The answer is found in Jesus' command to love one another.

Jesus of Nazareth is one of the most controversial figures in all of history. Countless people have been killed in his name, some for believing in him and others for choosing not to believe. He has been loved and hated. He has been followed with great devotion and has been criticized as a deceiver.

The conflict does not center around whether or not he actually existed. Historians settled that issue long ago. The battle surrounds his identity. Was he a prophet, teacher, Son of God, Messiah, Savior, or King? Some people believe he was some or all of those things.

I have my own personal convictions about Jesus.

I believe that he is God the Son, God in the flesh, one Person of the Trinity, co-equal with God the Father and God the Holy Spirit.

I believe that he gave up his life as a sacrifice to atone for mankind's rebellion against a loving God.

I believe that the only way to be right with God is through the forgiveness of sin made available by Jesus' sacrifice.

I believe that forgiveness, this grace that God offers, is completely unmerited and undeserved by our actions.

I didn't write this book to share my personal beliefs and convictions about who Jesus was or is. But I also don't want to be disingenuous about where I stand. Whether or not you share these beliefs, I think this book is for you. More specifically, I believe the challenges contained in this book are for you.

You see, despite all the discussion over the identity of Jesus, no one really argues with the teachings of Jesus. Seriously, in all my years as a pastor, I have never had anyone tell me they disagreed with the actual teachings of Jesus. Sure, some people disagree with some of the things they *think* he said. Or they might disagree with some of the things they *heard others claim* Jesus said. But when push comes to shove and we look at the actual firsthand accounts of his teaching and ministry, I have yet to have someone say that living and acting the way he taught is a bad idea.

"So now I am giving you a new commandment: Love each other," Jesus said (John 13:34).

Where is the controversy in that statement?

Islam, Buddhism, and Hinduism, three other major world religions, all esteem Jesus of Nazareth as a wise teacher.

Whether you approach Jesus Christ with curiosity and skepticism or with conviction, as your Savior, I believe you will benefit from this book.

Living out Jesus' command to love one another has the potential to dramatically impact your life. I am not talking about a feelings-based or emotional love here . . . and neither was Jesus. We are talking about an action-based love. A radical love that stretches the bounds of comfort and rational thinking. It's the kind of love that has the ability to change not only the relationships in your life but also the world itself.

But I'm getting ahead of myself.

We are going to take a look at five specific ways (in chapters 2 through 6) that Jesus instructs his followers to love. I am going to challenge you to try each one out, to put it into practice and see what happens. In each challenge we will break down a natural barrier in our life with an unnatural—or rather, supernatural—act of love. Over the course of the journey we will see what happens to the people you love and what happens to you in the process. In the last chapter we will catch a glimpse of what could happen if enough people choose to live out these challenges consistently.

You can read this book on your own and I believe it will be impactful. I also believe that if you read it with a group of friends, it has the power to be life-changing. I would encourage you to read a chapter each week and then meet together as a group to share how you are doing on the challenge, to learn from the experiences of others, and to encourage one another.

I am excited for you! I believe that living out the challenges of Jesus will be life-altering. If you take these challenges seriously each week, I believe it will be impossible not to experience the Jesus that I know.

Blessings,
Ryan Nunez

Chapter 1

The Command to Love

I invite you to participate in a Great Challenge.

There are a lot of them out there. It seems like people come up with more each day. Summiting Mt. Everest used to be the pinnacle of mountain climbing, but now it is climbing the highest peak on each continent. The Grand Canyon hike used to be a pretty big deal too, but just recently I had a friend do the rim-to-rim-to-rim challenge: he went down the canyon, up the other side, back down and up to his original starting point. Don't even get me started about running! I am a runner and have run a few marathons (26.2 miles, and don't forget the 0.2!), but now there are 50- and 100-mile trail runs.

Then there are the food challenges: eating super-hot ghost peppers without anything to drink, eating an entire 72 oz. steak in under an hour, and my kids' favorite: eating nasty-flavored jellybeans.

I have even seen a "husband does my makeup" challenge on YouTube where a woman allowed her husband to do her makeup and then posted a picture of the aftermath. She challenged others to do the same and share pictures as well.

Everyone loves a good challenge.

What if I told you that this challenge I am inviting you to take is 2,000 years old—and hasn't changed at all during that time? It hasn't been escalated. It hasn't become outdated. It is just as challenging today as it was when it was first given. Plus, you don't have to be in great physical shape or have a stomach of steel to do it.

And as an added bonus . . . I believe this challenge will change your life and the lives of those around you.

Let me tell you how I came to discover this Great Challenge.

I get great satisfaction in connecting dots. When I was young, this manifested itself in a significant amount of time spent with activity books, literally connecting the dots on paper. I loved those sheets, especially the ones where you had no idea what picture the dots were going to make until the very end.

I carried this passion for connecting the dots with me into adulthood. I enjoy seeing how things are related. Seeing the cause and effect of everything around us and discovering the underlying principles gives me that same satisfaction I experienced as a child.

That was probably one of the motivations behind my initial pursuit of a career in science. That *is* what being a scientist is all about, right?

In my academic career, I never discovered a natural law and I certainly didn't make any progress on a unified theory of everything. My contributions to science lie in a distant corner of Hayden Library at Arizona State University, where my dissertation is shelved. Four and a half years of graduate school and I was able to connect two dots in the field of material science. For that they gave me a Ph.D.!

That was a long time ago, and since then I have entered full-time ministry as a pastor. I've added a few seminary classes to my educational resume, and I have applied my love of connecting the dots to the faith I hold so dearly.

I make it a personal goal to read through the Bible every year. Some years I have a specific theme or study topic in mind. Other years I don't. As I was reading through the New Testament last year, I was trying to look at it through the eyes of someone who was skeptical about the whole thing. I intentionally tried to take off all the lenses I had acquired over the years that influence the way I read the Bible. I was attempting to get to the core of what the Scriptures were asking me to do—super practical stuff, the things checklists are made of.

Now please understand me: I do not believe authentically following Jesus can be reduced to a checklist. God desires a relationship with his children, not a transaction, but during this year's reading I was searching for a pattern.

Now, you might be a quicker study than I am. I like to connect the dots, but I never said I was very fast at it. It took me to the end of John's Gospel, the fourth book in the New Testament, to pick up on the pattern. I found it in Jesus' discussion with and prayer for his disciples the night before he was crucified:

> So now I am giving you a new commandment: Love each other. Just as I have loved you, you should love each other. Your love for one another will prove to the world that you are my disciples. (John 13:34–35)

This is the key to the pattern, where Jesus issues our Great Challenge. In that one statement Jesus says so much. It's a turning point. Here are four major observations.

1. This command is different than his previous commands.

2. He tells us how to love each other.

3. Jesus sets the example.

4. Our love is the evidence that we are his disciples.

To Jesus, loving each other is a *big* deal.

It doesn't stop there. Before the end of John's firsthand account of that evening, Jesus uses the word love thirty-two more times! He definitely wanted to make sure we understood he was saying something important.

After this realization I went back through the Gospels looking for Jesus' instructions on love. They weren't hard to find. In fact, over the course of a few weeks I re-read the entire New Testament and underlined every passage about love. I went through several yellow grease pencils.

These instructions on love were not just in the Gospel accounts. The early Church took these commands of Jesus and lived them out. The apostles' letters are full of encouragement and correction based on the way the early believers showed love.

The Apostle Paul wrote to the church in the city of Corinth: "Three things will last forever—faith, hope, and love—and the greatest of these is love" (1 Corinthians 13:13).

He also emphasized the importance of love to the church in Rome: "Owe nothing to anyone—except for your obligation to love one another" (13:8); and to the church in Galatia: "For you have been called to live in freedom, my brothers and sisters. But don't use your freedom to satisfy your sinful nature. Instead, use your freedom to serve one another in love" (5:13). And we can't forget his letters to the Christians in Ephesus, Philippi, Colossae, and Thessalonica, not to mention his personal letters to Philemon, Timothy, and Titus. They all call the early church communities to follow Jesus' command to love one another.

It's not just Paul, either. Peter says, "Most important of all, continue to show deep love for each other, for love covers a multitude of sins" (1 Peter 4:8). Phrases like "above all" and "most important" are connected with the commands of Christ to love.

How did I miss this?

I am not saying that I didn't know I am supposed to love others. I understood that loving others was important—just not *most* important. To be completely transparent, it's probably because I associate love primarily with a feeling, and I can't measure feelings. I can measure other stuff much more accurately. Like how much of the Bible I've read and how often, how long I pray, how often I fast, how many compliments I get when I preach or teach, and so on.

Sometimes I think God had me in mind specifically when he inspired Paul to write:

> If I could speak all the languages of earth and of angels, but didn't love others, I would only be a noisy gong or a clanging cymbal. If I had the gift of prophecy, and if I understood all of God's secret plans and possessed all knowledge, and if I had such faith that I could move mountains, but didn't love others, I would be nothing. If I gave everything I have to the poor and even sacrificed my body, I could boast about it; but if I didn't love others, I would have gained nothing. (1 Corinthians 13:1–3)

Without love I am nothing.

Does that mean that love is everything?

Jesus said something to that effect in response to the religious leaders of his day. They asked him which of the 613 commandments given in the Jewish Scriptures was the most important. Jesus responded:

"'You must love the LORD your God with all your heart, all your soul, and all your mind.' This is the first and greatest commandment. A second is equally important: 'Love your neighbor as yourself.' The entire law and all the demands of the prophets are based on these two commandments." (Matthew 22:37–40)

In summary, love God and love others. If you do that, you do everything else God has asked us to do as well.

That's the positive approach. I like the positive approach. By nature, I'm a glass-half-full kind of guy.

But to reinforce the importance of an action or a value, sometimes the "negative approach" is used too: what happens if I *don't* do the important thing? The Apostle John, Mr. Love himself, is clear that there are negative consequences of failing to love. He gives a stern warning to those who show a lack of love.

If we love our brothers and sisters who are believers, it proves that we have passed from death to life. But a person who has no love is still dead. Anyone who hates another brother or sister is really a murderer at heart. And you know that murderers don't have eternal life within them.

We know what real love is because Jesus gave up his life for us. So we also ought to give up our lives for our brothers and sisters. If someone has enough money to live well and sees a brother or sister in need but shows no compassion—how can God's love be in that person?

Dear children, let's not merely say that we love each other; let us show the truth by our actions. (1 John 3:14–18)

That is pretty tough! John is saying that if there is no love exhibited in your life, there is no evidence of God in your life.

To make sure we didn't miss his not-so-subtle hint, John comes out and says this a chapter later: "But anyone who does not love does not know God, for God is love" (1 John 4:8).

God is love.

If God is in you, love comes out of you. It's the proof.

Just to be clear, John drives us toward love that is action-oriented. This is not just a feeling or affection. We are not going to just sit around and talk about how much we love each other; it goes beyond that to something that can be seen by others.

I really like the way Eugene Peterson paraphrases this passage in his artistic interpretation of Scripture, *The Message*:

> The way we know we've been transferred from death to life is that we love our brothers and sisters. Anyone who doesn't love is as good as dead. Anyone who hates a brother or sister is a murderer, and you know very well that eternal life and murder don't go together.
>
> This is how we've come to understand and experience love: Christ sacrificed his life for us. This is why we ought to live sacrificially for our fellow believers, and not just be out for ourselves. If you see some brother or sister in need and have the means to do something about it but turn a cold shoulder and do nothing, what happens to God's love? It disappears. And you made it disappear.

My dear children, let's not just talk about love; let's practice real love. This is the only way we'll know we're living truly, living in God's reality.[1]

At this point, I believe we have a very solid case for love being a primary theme and command in Scripture. Of course, some readers—specifically you brave ones who are pursuing this challenge despite being a bit skeptical about Jesus, the Bible, and religion in general—were ready to get started in the introduction. I am laying this groundwork for the challenge to make sure we are all on the same page.

One of my pet peeves as a pastor is with a certain group of Christians. Specifically, Christians who complain that the teaching isn't deep enough. They somehow associate confusing topics, obscure Greek definitions, and complicated theological terminology with spiritual maturity. There is a tendency in the Christian world to dismiss a challenge like displaying love toward others as overly simplistic.

I could make it complicated. I could use Greek words and theological terms. I could make the book four times as long. But I am not going to. The Bible was written for everyone to understand. Across every time, and across every culture.

Think about that for a minute. The Bible was written for believers in the first century just as much as it was written for people in the twenty-first century. It is applicable to believers in remote villages in Côte d'Ivoire and metropolitan villages like Greenwich in New York City.

Simple does not mean shallow.

---

1. Peterson was a pastor and scholar who translated the original text of the Bible into contemporary English in order to bring its message to the people he served. My edition is Holy Bible: The Message, 2005, Colorado Springs, CO: NavPress.

Simple does not mean easy.

The Great Challenge is all about putting Jesus' command to love into practice. Our goal is to actually do what Jesus told his followers to do.

Not accidentally.

Not if the opportunity arises on its own.

The Great Challenge is about being intentional.

We do not have to wonder about how to live out Jesus' command to love one another. He told us how to do it. We are going to explore five commands from the teaching of Jesus that guide us through this challenge. Each command stretches us a bit further. Each one is progressively more difficult. This is Jesus' method.

When Jesus began gathering his disciples, the request was very simple: "Follow me." Philip's invitation to Nathanael was even simpler: "Come and see." That is a pretty low level of commitment. It's not a lot to ask someone to come and observe something or follow you around for a while. But that is not where Jesus left their commitment. Over time he asked for more. At one point, Jesus was talking to a wealthy young man whom he asked to sell everything in order to give the money to the poor. When the young man left sad, Jesus turned to his disciples and raised the bar, telling them that they need to love him more than possessions. Later on, Jesus tells his disciples that they need to love him so much that in comparison it seems like they hate their own families. Here he raises the bar again: I need to be your most important relationship. Finally, toward the end of his ministry Jesus tells his followers that they must deny themselves, pick up their crosses, and follow him. They must love him more than their own life. The bar doesn't get any higher than that!

Look at the progression.

How many disciples do you think Jesus would have had if he started with the call to the cross? I don't know for sure, but my guess would be south of the number twelve.

As they spend more time with Jesus, learning to trust him, the disciples are ready for bigger and bigger commitments. We will follow that same pattern with our challenges.

Jesus' specific commands to love form the outline of this challenge. I am not going to challenge you to do anything that Jesus himself does not ask all his followers to do.

Here is what Jesus told us to do:

Love everyone regardless of position.

Jesus was very clear with his disciples that in his kingdom, leaders serve. The rest of the world might serve leaders and those in authority, but Jesus set the example of servant leadership.

And since I, your Lord and Teacher, have washed your feet, you ought to wash each other's feet. I have given you an example to follow. Do as I have done to you (John 13:14–15).

The trap of privilege, or a feeling of entitlement, is a destructive mindset. You will always live in disappointment with your expectations never met. You will also constantly strive for more, hoping the next level of recognition—and then the next, and the next—will bring you the fulfillment you desire. This ultimately leads to isolation because you view people as objects to fulfill your desires. When we love everyone regardless of position, we are overcoming privilege with service to others.

Love sacrificially.

Jesus called us to a love that costs us something. A sacrificial love that puts the other person's needs ahead of our own.

There is no greater love than to lay down one's life for one's friends (John 15:13).

Our natural tendency is to "look out for number one," and make sure we take care of ourselves. This is, in a word, selfishness. Selfishness is a barrier to authentic relationships. No relationship can grow without giving of yourself. When we love sacrificially, we are overcoming selfishness with generosity.

Love those different than you.

It's easy to demonstrate love to your friends and to people who can return the favor. Everyone does that. What is special is when you demonstrate love to someone different than you or someone who is unable to pay you back.

Love your neighbor as yourself (Matthew 22:39).

The follow-up question to this conversation in the Gospel of Luke was, "Who is my neighbor?" Jesus responded by telling one of his most famous parables, about the least likely neighbors (Luke 10:30-37). The parable showcases ethnic divides, religious divides, political divides, and an extreme act of compassion. When we love those different than us, we overcome bias with compassion.

Love the difficult to love.

Some situations make us nervous. I am not talking about being scared for your safety; I'm talking about being around people who are really struggling, people who are homeless, people who are dealing with mental illness, prisoners. What is our responsibility to them?

I tell you the truth, when you did it to one of the least of these my brothers and sisters, you were doing it to me! (Matthew 25:40).

We probably won't be able to fix all the problems around us with an act of love, but we can bridge a gap that should not exist between two people created in God's image. When we love those who are difficult to love, we overcome fear with presence.

Love your enemy.

This is the big one. Jesus turned the crowd's perceptions upside down with this statement.

But I say, love your enemies! (Matthew 5:44).

But how, Jesus? Don't you know what they did? Don't you know how much it hurt? They haven't even said they were sorry. They didn't even acknowledge my pain. It's not fair!

Our anger at someone who hurts us or a loved one is real. It may be justified. And sometimes it feels kind of good. But the problem is that over time it eats you up inside. Anger limits your ability to connect with others. It creates a wall between you and the world. When we love our enemies, we overcome anger with forgiveness.

———

To love as Jesus called us to love is an amazing challenge. It is one that will impact and influence the lives of those we encounter, but it will also impact us. Jesus said, "The thief's purpose is to steal and kill and destroy. My purpose is to give them a rich and satisfying life" (John 10:10).

How will our lives be different if we choose to love others in this way? Will our lives become rich and satisfying?

Loving others the way Jesus asks will allow us to address some of the greatest causes of pain and division in our lives: privilege, selfishness, bias, fear, and anger. Every time I respond by acting in love, a little more selfishness is removed from my life, a little bias is broken down, a little anger goes away. The ultimate result is relational health. The things that cause division in my relationships are slowly taken away by acts of love. My family becomes more unified. My work environment becomes healthier.

Imagine for a moment what this would do in your church. It could create a unity and peace that make the church an attractive light in your community.

Let's think even bigger. What if the Christians from different churches in your community started treating one another with the type of love Jesus commanded? What if we weren't so concerned about what "brand" of Christian we are and instead viewed one another primarily as brothers and sisters in Christ? I am not talking about making one church and dissolving denominations. Unity does not mean uniformity. I am talking about working together and getting along. What impact would that have on your community?

On the first Thursday of every month, I sit down with two pastors from churches that are not in my denomination. We have coffee, talk about our personal lives and our ministries, and pray for one another. We text each other all the time. We offer advice when we're asked—and sometimes when we're not. We don't do this because we are part of the same organization or denomination. It's simply because we are friends. Because of the churches we pastor, the fact that we are friends is extremely unusual.

Dan and Samson speak in tongues. I do not.

Samson is a preacher. Dan and I are teachers.

I am introverted. Dan is the most extraverted person I know.

We all fall on different spots of the Calvin-Arminian spectrum.

We are a walking joke: A Baptist pastor, a Charismatic pastor, and an inner-city pastor walk into a bar. Just kidding—the Baptist pastor waited in the car.

We could debate theology for the rest of our lives and never run out of differences to discuss. We are definitely from different Christian tribes. But that never comes up. It's not because we don't hold our beliefs and convictions with passion. It's because we love each other as brothers in Christ. Our love for each other has created a unity among us that's incredible. It's the relational rock that keeps me emotionally healthy. It has also created the foundation for the largest cooperative effort of churches in the West Valley of Phoenix.

Out of our friendship has come Better Together. Its mission is to form healthy leaders to lead healthy churches, bringing health to local communities. Several times a year, more than one hundred pastors and ministry leaders from different churches and denominations come together for fellowship, encouragement, and equipping. We get away together for prayer retreats. We work together on School Connect, which is a collaboration of churches, businesses, and government agencies working together to meet the needs of local schools. We are well on our way to having every school in our county adopted by a local church.

Sometimes I dare to dream even bigger than that.

Amazing things happen when we choose to love one another.

At the end of the day, this is not a top-down change. It starts with individual followers of Jesus living out the command to love one another. I invite you along to join this Great Challenge. Let's see how God might choose to work *through* his followers. Let's see how God might choose to work *in* his followers.

Chapter 2

Love Regardless of Position

When my wife Adrienne and I were in college we both had jobs at a structural engineering firm. She worked in the billing office and I worked in the print room doing deliveries, and eventually assisting the engineers. I was on scholarship at Arizona State University, so this job paid for books, insurance, gas, and occasionally dinner with Adrienne at a place nicer than Taco Bell. But this story is not about me.

Adrienne did not have a scholarship. She needed this job to pay her way through nursing school. (You could actually do that back then!) If she budgeted well, saved over the summers, and worked during school breaks she could pay for her tuition each semester.

This went well for a while . . . until it didn't. An unexpected expense came up and the money she was saving for the next semester's bill was gone. Adrienne was stressed.

It wasn't hopeless. There were other options—student loans, credit cards. She wasn't going to drop out of school. She just needed a new plan.

That's when Paul walked into her office. Paul was one of the owners of the engineering firm. He heard about Adrienne's dilemma and offered a solution. He offered to pay the full bill for her tuition that semester. She would then pay half of it back in hours at work and the other half would be a gift.

Did I mention it was nursing school? Why would an engineering firm pay for one of its part-time employees to get a job elsewhere?

Paul did this every semester until she graduated and took her first nursing job. She walked into her first day of work at St. Joseph's Hospital without student loans and carrying the nicest designer bag of any recent graduate—courtesy of the owners of the engineering firm.

Whenever I tell this story the reaction is usually the same: a warm smile spreads across the listener's face. A few times there has been a comment like "Wow!" or "How generous." But most of the time it's simply a smile. Why does this story always resonate with people?

I believe it is because we were created to use our resources for the benefit of others. Why, you might ask? Because that is what God is like. We are created in God's image, so when we act in alignment with his character or see someone else doing so, we don't have to be told . . . we just know it's right.

What takes it to the next level is the unrequited nature of this particular act. It makes business sense for an engineering company to help an *engineering* student through school. This young woman or man could eventually become an asset to the company. The owners would build loyalty through their generosity.

When someone uses their position of power and influence to help others less fortunate or vulnerable, we celebrate it. We make movies. We write songs. We love that story!

We just don't see it that often.

You see, our natural tendency is to use any influence or power we might have to help ourselves.

It seems like every day the news is full of accounts of abuse by the powerful: governments, corporations and the executives who run them, producers and movie stars, even teachers, clergy, and parents.

When we leverage our influence for our own benefit, we cause pain, destruction, trauma, and division. We know this is not the way to live, but how do we change our course?

Certain passages in the Bible make me think to myself, why would the writer include that? I mean, it kind of makes them all look bad. Accounts like King David's affair and Peter's denial of knowing Jesus show flaws in the biblical saints. You don't have to read far to see that our biblical heroes are far from perfect.

This vulnerability is rare in ancient writing. These passages remind me that the Bible is more than just an ancient book. It is not a biography written to paint the writers or the figures in the accounts as heroes. It's about God's great plan of redemption. It is about how to live in God's kingdom.

As we read through the Gospel accounts we follow along with the disciples as they are learning. One of the lessons that comes up over and over concerns their struggle with privilege.

The writer of the Gospel of Mark was not one of the twelve disciples; he was a companion of Peter after Pentecost. This Gospel contains Peter's firsthand account of the life and ministry of Jesus.

> After they arrived at Capernaum and settled in a house, Jesus asked his disciples, "What were you discussing out on the road?" But they didn't answer, because they had been arguing about which of them was the greatest. He sat down, called the twelve disciples over to him, and said, "Whoever wants to be first must take last place and be the servant of everyone else." (Mark 9:33–35)

How embarrassing! Caught red-handed! Of course they didn't want to answer, because this was not the first time this issue of privilege and position had come up.

Jesus preached it in the Beatitudes. He illustrated it by bringing children to the front of the crowd. He taught the principle in private to the disciples.

It was hard for them to grasp and internalize Jesus' attitude toward privilege because most of the disciples were experiencing these temptations for the first time. We don't know what every disciple did before following Jesus, but the core group—Peter, James, John, and Andrew—were fishermen. It wasn't a bad job, but they certainly had little opportunity to exercise power and authority over others.

As Jesus' ministry grew and thousands began showing up wherever he went, the Twelve began to see the possibilities.

The disciples believed that Jesus was the Messiah. The people were hoping that he was the Messiah. To fully understand Jesus' growing influence, one must understand what "Messiah" ("anointed one") meant to Jews in the first century.

At this point the Jewish people had been living under foreign rule for over seven hundred years. Because of their rebellion against God—their inability to follow his commands and worship only him—God had allowed foreign nations to conquer and rule the Jews. It's not as though they weren't warned. Prophet after prophet was sent to call the people back to God: Elijah, Elisha, Joel, Amos . . . this list goes on. Sometimes the people would temporarily return to God. Other times the prophet was ignored entirely.

The first to conquer the Jews were the Assyrians, then the Babylonians, followed by the Persians, Greeks, and finally the Romans, which is where they now stood.

Because of this near-constant occupation, when first-century Jews thought about the Messiah, they pictured a literal—and usually militant—king. They read all the promises of the prophets through this lens.

> Rejoice, O people of Zion!
>> Shout in triumph, O people of Jerusalem!
> Look, your king is coming to you.
> He is righteous and victorious,
> yet he is humble, riding on a donkey—
>> riding on a donkey's colt. . . .
> [And] your king will bring peace to the nations.
> His realm will stretch from sea to sea
>> and from the Euphrates River to the
>> ends of the earth.
>
> (Zechariah 9:9–10)

Zechariah's message surely meant that they were finally going to be rid of the Romans, that the Messiah would be their earthly king who would rule with perfect justice, and peace would reign.

If there were to be a king and a kingdom, as Jesus' disciples believed, the natural question became, where did they fit in? Obviously Jesus would be in charge, but he would probably need some help from regional kings and governors. I am sure their imaginations ran wild, especially considering their humble beginnings. Who would have thought that a bunch of fishermen from Galilee could have so much influence?

The disciples were not the only ones thinking this way. Behind every ambitious young man is a proud mother.

> Then the mother of James and John, the sons of Zebedee, came to Jesus with her sons.
>
> She knelt respectfully to ask a favor. "What is your request?" he asked.

She replied, "In your Kingdom, please let my two sons sit in places of honor next to you, one on your right and the other on your left."

But Jesus answered by saying to them, "You don't know what you are asking! Are you able to drink from the bitter cup of suffering I am about to drink?"

"Oh yes," they replied, "we are able!"

Jesus told them, "You will indeed drink from my bitter cup. But I have no right to say who will sit on my right or my left. My Father has prepared those places for the ones he has chosen."

When the ten other disciples heard what James and John had asked, they were indignant. But Jesus called them together and said, "You know that the rulers in this world lord it over their people, and officials flaunt their authority over those under them. But among you it will be different. Whoever wants to be a leader among you must be your servant, and whoever wants to be first among you must become your slave. For even the Son of Man came not to be served but to serve others and to give his life as a ransom for many." (Matthew 20:20–28)

It's a pretty ugly scene, isn't it? We see the disciples jockeying for position and going behind each others' backs; we see how easily jealousy and division arise among even this tightly knit group.

It seems like it comes back to that a lot, doesn't it? When privilege, power, and influence are used selfishly, division inevitably makes an appearance.

Jesus says it again: My kingdom is different than the examples you see. We will not be operating under the system you see demonstrated around you every day, the system that victimizes you. This is going to be radical. Instead of gaining influence to get payback, to get the things you always wanted, we are going to use those positions to serve others. We are going to use authority and privilege to help others, not ourselves. And I [Jesus] am going to show you how.

The struggle of privilege takes many forms. I have seen it rear its ugly head in several different ways during my life so far.

I grew up in the West Valley of Phoenix. My two brothers and I were raised primarily by our single mom. We always had enough food and we always had a roof over our heads, but things were always tight. I often saw my mom struggling. She ran a little daycare out of her basement and I always remember the end of each week just kind of waiting for all the parents to pay her. She would then head off to the bank to make the deposit, and I was stressed out watching her.

My mom never talked about finances. She never *said* she was stressed, but you could see it, you could feel the tension. I know the church stepped in a couple of times to help in emergencies. We had a great support system. But I just didn't want to be in that situation. So I promised myself that I would get a degree and a good job so that I would be financially set. I was going to make sure that I put in the work so that I would always have what I need and be able to take care of myself. I was going to get myself in a position to be comfortable.

Honestly what I was really doing was setting myself up for a life of privilege. I got the good grades to earn a scholarship for school. I worked hard to get a degree, and another degree. I wanted to set myself apart. Then, I decided, I would deserve all the promotions and pay raises in my career.

Privilege, or entitlement, can take multiple forms. There are the people who do nothing and expect everything to happen for them, and there are people who work really hard and expect everything to happen for them. Both are self-centered. Neither reflects God's image.

There are other conditions that can lead to privilege. I am most vulnerable to pursuing privilege when I am tired and worn out. I am sure you've been there too. It's the end of a long day, or week, or quarter, and you have given it all you had. You tell yourself, I deserve an indulgence. I've earned it.

That's when I find myself in a burrito coma regretting my poor choices.

Sometimes it's overconfidence. When you are in a role of positional authority, as a school principal, manager, military leader, supervisor, government official, pastor, or executive, people will often go out of their way to encourage you and tell you how great you are. After a while you believe the hype. You buy into all the great things that people are saying and you develop an overinflated view of yourself. Or it could just be regular old pride; you know, the pride that causes us to seek out recognition and believe that we're kind of a big deal. Self-serving privilege.

Paul pulls no punches in his letter to the Christians in Philippi: Jesus was very clear that there was no room in his kingdom for self-serving leaders.

> Don't be selfish; don't try to impress others. Be humble, thinking of others as better than yourselves. Don't look out only for your own interests, but take an interest in others, too.

You must have the same attitude that Christ Jesus had.
Though he was God,
> he did not think of equality with God
> as something to cling to.

Instead, he gave up his divine privileges;
> he took the humble position of a slave
> and was born as a human being.
When he appeared in human form,
> he humbled himself in obedience to God
> and died a criminal's death on a cross.

Therefore, God elevated him to the place of
> highest honor and gave him the name
> above all other names,
that at the name of Jesus every knee should bow,
> in heaven and on earth and under the earth,

and every tongue declare that Jesus Christ is Lord,
> to the glory of God the Father.

(Philippians 2:3–11)

The Gospel accounts of the night of Jesus' betrayal are rich with his teaching. Knowing that he was going to be crucified the next day, Jesus spent the evening with the disciples wrapping up three years of mentoring. The teachings he emphasizes are those closest to his heart and to his will for us.

One might guess that privilege in God's kingdom came up. But this time it wasn't a talk or sermon. It wasn't a response to conversation. It was an object lesson.

Jesus spent this last evening celebrating Passover, the Jewish festival celebrating God's deliverance of his people from slavery in Egypt. Passover signifies the final plague levied on the Egyptians, which killed all firstborn sons throughout the kingdom. But God's judgment *passed over* each Israelite household covered by the blood of a lamb.

God instructed his people to celebrate this festival every year to remember what he had done for them.

As Jesus and the disciples reached the upper room where preparations had been made for the celebration, Jesus got a towel and some water and began to wash the disciples' feet.

The washing of feet was a widespread custom in this region. Sandaled feet got very dirty. They walked alongside animals in the dirt, mud, and dust. Getting all that off your feet before you entered into a house was more comfortable for everyone. It was a sign of your host's hospitality toward you and of your respect toward them.

It was so customary to have your feet washed when invited into a home that it was pretty much a given. But it would never be expected that the man of the house do the washing; it was a job for servants. (Remember what was on those feet!)

It is hard for us to comprehend how shocking this scene would have been for the disciples. Jesus, the Messiah, was washing their feet. At this point they still believed that Jesus was going to be an actual earthly king. Kings do not wash their subjects' feet.

Or do they?

The more Jesus talks about the kingdom of God, the more upside down it appears.

Jesus was *the* master teacher. You've probably had a few great teachers in your past. They didn't just lecture; they demonstrated. Whether it was an experiment in a science class or a connection between a book you were reading and the historical movement it started, great teachers led you to that "Aha!" moment that solidified the concept.

That's what Jesus was doing when he washed their feet.

After washing their feet, he put on his robe again and sat down and asked, "Do you understand what I was doing? You call me 'Teacher' and 'Lord,' and you are right, because that's what I am. And since I, your Lord and Teacher, have washed your feet, you ought to wash each other's feet. **I have given you an example to follow. Do as I have done to you.**" (John 13:12–15, emphasis added)

Jesus has given us the antidote to privileged living.

Typically, when we are talking about antidotes we are referring to a physical problem. An antidote counteracts poison and takes away its harmful effects. As I mentioned before, my family and I live in Arizona, and almost everyone I know here has come across a scorpion.

Interesting fact: the more one gets stung by a scorpion, the more severe the reaction is.

We discovered this when my wife was stung for the third time. This time it was on the inside of her forearm. The pain was much greater than before and the numbing started to spread. As the toxin spread through her body we began to be concerned.

We came up with a plan. For most stings one needs only a dose of Benadryl , but there is an antidote available for severe cases. So we would go to the ER parking lot and wait. If the symptoms didn't get worse, we would just drive home with our co-pay still in our checking account. But if they got worse, we'd walk in and get the help she needed.

As we sat in the car waiting it out, I looked over at Adrienne and noticed something funny. It was her eyes. They were spinning. Not in the same direction. They looked like the eyes of a cartoon character who had been hit in the head with a hammer.

We went inside.

As I said, an antidote counteracts poison and takes away its harmful effects. When Jesus gave the command to serve one another, he was writing the prescription to cure self-serving attitudes. The only way we can break selfishness is to serve.

Let's not mistake Jesus' tone, either. This was not a suggestion or aspiration. This was a command. If you are going to be a part of his kingdom, this is what you will do.

Over the course of this book we are going to examine five specific commands Jesus gives us. Each one requires taking on a specific challenge. You see, to follow the commands of Jesus takes some intentionality. We don't just find ourselves accidentally serving others. We make choices to do so. And the more we intentionally set out to serve, the more natural it becomes. "Physical training is good, but training for godliness is much better, promising benefits in this life and in the life to come" (1 Timothy 4:8).

As we take intentional steps to serve and love others in the way that Jesus taught and demonstrated, we will begin to see the fruit of this type of living. Relationships strengthen. Our character is developed. Our dependence on Christ increases. These challenges are difficult and will get progressively more so. If we are relying on ourselves to rise to the challenge, we will be disappointed. We might be able to do it every once in a while, but by developing a dependence on God so that his strength and power can begin working through us, the challenges become possible on a regular basis.

Challenge #1

Demonstrate love to someone over whom you have influence or authority.

For this chapter's challenge you don't have to go far to find the person to whom you will demonstrate love because you already know them. They are currently in your life. However, depending on your vocation and general stage of life, it might be more challenging to specifically identify someone over whom you have influence or authority.

Let's start with a few general categories.

In a family, parents and grandparents have their children and grandchildren. Aunts and uncles have nieces and nephews. Older siblings have younger siblings.

In a business environment there are many inherent levels of influence. You don't have to be the CEO to be able to demonstrate love to someone under your authority. Directors, managers, supervisors, shift leaders, and team leaders all have people under their influence. Whether one person or a thousand work under your authority, you have an opportunity to love in this way.

Every teacher has students. You could be at the head of a university lab, high school sports team, fourth grade classroom, church class, coffee shop Bible study, or neighborhood book club.

Military units and government offices have a natural hierarchy.

If you are having trouble thinking of anyone, or narrowing it down to a specific person, ask God. I know it might sound like a cliché, especially if you are a bit skeptical about things like that. But give it a try. What do you have to lose? I truly believe God answers prayer and when we sincerely ask for help he will give it.

Now that you have a person in mind, come up with a plan to demonstrate love to them this week. Quick tip: I would probably not go with the foot-washing thing. It's not really part of our culture and would just weird them out.

It doesn't have to be extravagant. It just needs to demonstrate love to that person. Finding a specific need to fill might be a good way to start.

A friend of mine from my small group recently met this challenge by cooking a meal for a woman at work whose husband was out of town. The woman has several young children and she was getting worn out. A meal met a specific need for that family and spoke love to the mother, who got a little break from cooking for the evening.

You could also write a word of encouragement to someone. Drop off a meaningful small gift. Provide an evening of childcare for a young family. Get creative. Let the needs drive you to action.

The point of the challenge is to be intentional. This will require us to step out of our comfort zones. These acts of service will affect the people you choose. A genuine demonstration of love will impact them in ways you may never fully understand.

Serving in this way will also leave a mark on you. When we demonstrate love in this way, we move from a position of privilege to one of service. As we continue to do this it will not just change the outlook of your day or week. It will change your character. When we move from a heart of privilege to a heart of serving we more accurately reflect the heart of God.

Chapter 3

Love Sacrificially

As a father of four children, I don't have time for many hobbies. However, one thing I really enjoy doing is running. I have been running consistently since I graduated from high school. Each morning I get up early before the rest of the family to get my run in.

I have always been self-conscious about calling myself a runner because I have never had any training or instruction. I didn't run track or cross country in high school, so I've never had a coach. And I am not very fast. I simply decided one day to start running and I never stopped.

Over the years I entered some races and completed several marathons. I still was not fast . . . but I could run for a long time. By nature I am also frugal, so I always got my running shoes at the outlet mall. I got good shoes, just not the current model. I have had some crazy shoe colors over the years, but hey, they were a good deal. All of this to the pain of my wife's good sense of style.

Eventually, my wife convinced me to go to the actual running shoe store. Evidently, that's where all the current models are sold, along with the normal colors. However, the moment I arrived at the shop, all that insecurity about being a "real runner" bubbled up inside me. The salesperson was an *actual* runner. He knew what he was talking about and was asking me questions that I had no answers for. Get me back to the outlet mall with the sixteen-year-old kid who knows nothing about distance running, I thought!

Finally, we settled on a shoe to try on and he went to the back to get my size. What a relief, I thought. This ordeal is almost over; all the questions and perceived judgment will end.

He returned and handed me the new shoe. I reached down, placed it on my foot, and quickly tied up the laces.

"You are doing it wrong," the salesman immediately said.

I looked up in confusion, trying to register what I had just done that could possibly be wrong. Had he secretly watched video of my last marathon? I was still staring at him perplexed when he said it again: "You are doing it wrong."

Another awkward pause.

"Your laces, you tied them wrong."

"Oh, sorry," I said as I untied them and slowly retied the knot.

"Wrong," he said again.

I cannot remember how many times I tied the same knot and got the same response. It seemed like forever, and I imagined that everyone in the shop was watching me fail at tying my shoes (it was kindergarten all over again). Eventually he put an end to the madness and asked if I would like him to show me the correct way, and I agreed.

He carefully bent down and tied a knot very similar to mine, but with one extra loop. "There," he said, "that knot will stay together like the double knot you have been tying, but look here, just pull on the end of the lace and it comes undone easily."

I pulled on the end of the lace and sure enough, it came right undone. He guided me through the process several more times before I was able to tie it correctly on my own.

Undoing thirty-five years of muscle memory and uncon-
scious skill is not easy. But do you know, it was a better way
to tie my shoe.

As I reflected later on this trying event, I couldn't help
but smile. This man didn't give me a new set of laces. He was
not trying to sell me a special shoelace product. He was simply showing me a different way to use what I already had.
And at the end of the day, it wasn't even all that different.
The tying process was still the same: crosses, loops, tucks,
pulls . . . he just gave me a different combination.

This got me thinking about Jesus.

When Jesus started his public ministry, he was criticized by the religious leaders of the day for turning people
away from the law that God had given their ancestors. Jesus
responded by saying, "Don't misunderstand why I have
come. I did not come to abolish the law of Moses or the
writings of the prophets. No, I came to accomplish their
purpose" (Matthew 5:17).

He wasn't taking away God's standards and laws; he
was showing the people God's original intention. He was
showing them a new way to live in relationship with God. A
better way. A more fulfilling way.

The Sermon on the Mount is recorded in the Gospel
of Matthew. In it, Jesus takes the time to explain what it
looks like to live in the kingdom of God. This sermon was
not taught just once—it was taught many times to many
different audiences. As Jesus traveled from town to town
and village to village, this was the message he brought.

In his teaching, Jesus points his audience over and over
to the kingdom of heaven. Jesus uses the phrase kingdom of
heaven, or kingdom of God, to explain the changes that are
happening with a concept everyone understood.

Let's look at the basics of a kingdom: Kingdoms are ruled by a sovereign ruler, or king. Every kingdom has boundaries to which the king's authority extends. People living within the boundaries of the kingdom fall under the king's authority and are expected to live under his rules as his subjects. A good king protects and provides for his subjects.

Even though I don't live in a kingdom ruled by a king, and you most likely don't either, the concepts are still easy to understand. The ministry of Jesus focuses on the fact that the kingdom of heaven is near—not here yet, but coming soon—and you need to be prepared.

Jesus wanted his followers to understand that his Father was not like the earthly kings they had encountered or heard of. God was certainly not like Caesar, their Roman emperor. The stories that Jesus told painted pictures of what God, our King, is like.

He is like a shepherd who searches for his lost sheep.

He is like a father who welcomes home and forgives his rebellious son.

He is like a manager who entrusts his servants with resources to manage.

This was a very different kind of King. God genuinely cares for his people. He loves and forgives. He trusts and rewards. In fact, the entire concept seems completely upside down compared to the kingdoms of the world. People's heads must have been spinning as Jesus described, with authority, this new reality.

The way in which God expects us to live is different as well. The general expectation for living in a kingdom is that one follows the rules set out by the king. If your actions match up with the expectations, you will be allowed to continue living in the kingdom. If your actions don't match up, meaning you choose to rebel against the king, the consequences will be swift and severe. In order to fully describe the kingdom of heaven, Jesus spends time teaching about the expectations. If the crowds were not completely rocked by Jesus' description of what God was like, they definitely would be when he described his expectations for subjects of the kingdom.

In Jesus' teaching about kingdom expectations, he makes dramatic use of the phrase, "you have heard." Jesus starts with the laws given by God through their ancestor Moses. They had been living by these laws for over a thousand years. You could almost say that these laws were their identity. The people related to God through the laws, and if they followed the laws, all 613 of them, they would receive God's blessing. If they didn't, that's when bad things would begin to happen. The new reality of God's kingdom coming to earth was changing the dynamic of these expectations. Some people have stated incorrectly that all these rules were just erased, but that's not quite true. Jesus did change the expectation, but instead of erasing the rules, he actually raised the bar.

Here is an example: "You have heard the commandment that says, 'You must not commit adultery.' But I say, anyone who even looks at a woman with lust has already committed adultery with her in his heart" (Matthew 5:27–28).

In this passage Jesus points back to the familiar command from the Ten Commandments: "You must not commit adultery" (Exodus 20:14). This is a pretty straightforward actions-based rule. Either you did or you did not have sex with someone who was not your spouse. There is not a whole lot of gray area.

However, in God's kingdom there is a higher standard. God cares about our actions, but he also cares about our hearts. Every action we take starts inside us. The new standard is to draw the line at lust, daydreaming, internal dialogues . . .

you get the picture. God doesn't want subjects in his kingdom doing the right things with their actions, but then walking around fantasizing and thinking of all the evil they would like to do. God wants *all* of us . . . starting with our hearts.

Jesus also demonstrates the same change when it comes to loving others.

Showing love to other people was not a new concept to the people of God. The Jews refer to the first five books of Scripture as the Torah, or Law. It was in one of these books, Leviticus, that the command to love was encoded in the Jewish law: "Do not seek revenge or bear a grudge against a fellow Israelite, but love your neighbor as yourself. I am the LORD" (Leviticus 19:18).

Love your neighbor as yourself. It is such a common saying now that we see it everywhere. It's been reworded and relabeled as the Golden Rule. You will see it posted in public school classrooms and you can even get a special edition license plate in Arizona with the phrase on it. It has become so prolific many people don't even associate it with the Bible anymore. A lot of people think it's a Benjamin Franklin quote!

Because of its familiarity today, we often don't realize how radical this statement was at the time.

When God gave this instruction to Moses the prevailing attitude was not, "Do unto others as you *want* them to do unto you." It was "Do unto others as they *have done* unto you." This wasn't just a feeling or belief; it was recorded and distributed by ancient Israel's near neighbors. One of the oldest surviving examples of ancient writing is Hammurabi's Code. Hammurabi was an ancient Babylonian ruler who recorded the laws of his kingdom along with the consequences for breaking them. The statement "an eye for an eye" from Hammurabi's Code describes the type of justice and expectations that were prevalent during this time.

The rules and expectations God gave the Israelites set them apart from their neighbors. They were God's chosen people whom he would use to unfold his amazing plan of redemption for all mankind. Loving just like everyone else did was not sufficient. God called his people to love others like they themselves wanted to be loved.

With the focus on treating others as you want to be treated, the scope of the command naturally grew. When we reflect on how we want to be loved, we often go back to a time when we were not shown love and think how we would have liked to have been treated instead. This becomes a new challenge for us. The Israelites, as a people, shared some collective experiences that expanded the way they lived this out.

> Always remember that you were slaves in Egypt and that the LORD your God redeemed you from your slavery. That is why I have given you this command.
>
> When you are harvesting your crops and forget to bring in a bundle of grain from your field, don't go back to get it. Leave it for the foreigners, orphans, and widows. Then the LORD your God will bless you in all you do. When you beat the olives from your olive trees, don't go over the boughs twice. Leave the remaining olives for the foreigners, orphans, and widows. (Deuteronomy 24:18–20)

If the Israelites didn't stand out from the cultures around them before, they sure did now. But it was more than just some crops left in the fields. Foreigners, widows, and orphans were specifically ensured justice, given food allotments, and invited into festival celebrations.

Love others as you love yourself.

As Jesus taught about the kingdom of heaven, he raised the standard of each command from rules based on our actions to expectations of our heart condition. So what did Jesus do with this command? It's already pretty radical! When it comes to "love your neighbor as yourself," how could the standard get higher than this? The part of the command that specifies "as you love yourself" already makes it a command of the heart.

But Jesus does raise the expectation.

We previously looked at the example Jesus set by washing the disciples' feet on the night that he was betrayed. Jesus was driving home the point that in the kingdom of God those who have authority and influence should use it to serve and love others. This was the first challenge of the book: love everyone regardless of position.

From the scene of the washing of the feet, we enter into the longest recorded monologue of Jesus. By now the theme should not be surprising: it is love. Jesus talks about the love we need to have for each other, the love he has for the Father, the love the Father has for him, the love the Father and the Son have for us, and the love that unites us all. Jesus is so loving that he is able to have this talk with his disciples even though he knows one of them has betrayed him.

He starts it all off with a statement that at first is a little bit confusing: "So now I am giving you a new commandment: Love each other. Just as I have loved you, you should love each other" (John 13:34).

How is this a new commandment? "Love each other" sounds just like the old commandment. The only difference is that Jesus added, "Just as I have loved you, you should love each other." So what difference does that make?

In a word: Everything.

The example to follow in loving others is now Jesus himself. We are to love others as he loved us. This is why the command is new. The old command, "love your neighbor as yourself," has been replaced with, "love each other as I loved you." It is now no longer good enough to use myself as the standard for treating others. Jesus' love is now the standard.

My love, even for myself, has limits. Jesus' love has no limits. *His love is eternal*

Jesus gave this command knowing full well what would happen very shortly. That night he would be turned over to the religious and Roman authorities and sentenced to death for crimes he did not commit. He submitted willingly to the cross knowing that by giving up his life, he would make forgiveness available for all.

Jesus called us to a love that costs us something. A sacrificial love that puts the other people's needs ahead of our own. "There is no greater love than to lay down one's life for one's friends" (John 15:13).

Love was always the motivation. Earlier in Jesus' ministry, he has an incredible conversation with a religious leader. This leader, named Nicodemus, was a Pharisee, but he was honestly seeking the truth about who Jesus was. Late one night, under the cover of darkness, Jesus told him why he was sent: "For this is how God loved the world: He gave his one and only Son, so that everyone who believes in him will not perish but have eternal life" (John 3:16).

Love was the reason God sent the Son. Since love was the motivation for Jesus' sacrifice, that same sacrifice serves as the ultimate example of love. "We know what real love is because Jesus gave up his life for us. So we also ought to give up our lives for our brothers and sisters" (1 John 3:16).

The new command is to love sacrificially. We should love in a way that costs us something.

The difficulty in living this way is that it is not natural. Our natural tendency is to make sure we take care of ourselves. In a word, this is selfishness. Selfishness is what we are fighting against when it comes to sacrificial love.

The early Church took to heart the command of Jesus to love sacrificially. We see this demonstrated in the book of Acts of the Apostles, where we get a firsthand look at what the early Church actually did.

After Jesus' resurrection, he promised his followers that the Holy Spirit would soon arrive and empower them to take the gospel message to everyone everywhere. On the day of Pentecost that promise was fulfilled. This group of about 120 of Jesus' closest followers went from hiding for their lives to preaching boldly in the streets of Jerusalem. The Holy Spirit gave them the gift to communicate with power, authority, and understanding to all who were present that day. It is recorded that on that day over three thousand people became followers of Jesus and were baptized. The Church was birthed that day.

Unfortunately for the leaders, Jesus didn't leave a manual for them to follow. How often were they were supposed to meet? How should they organize and govern? What were worship services supposed to look like? But perhaps it was in the divine plan that they didn't have a manual, because what they ended up doing was letting Jesus' commands to love guide their actions and focus.

All the believers devoted themselves to the apostles' teaching, and to fellowship, and to sharing in meals (including the Lord's Supper), and to prayer.

A deep sense of awe came over them all, and the apostles performed many miraculous signs and wonders. And all the believers met together in one place and shared everything they had. They sold their property and possessions and shared the money with those in need. They worshiped together at the Temple each day, met in homes for the Lord's Supper, and shared their meals with great joy and generosity—all the while praising God and enjoying the goodwill of all the people. And each day the Lord added to their fellowship those who were being saved. (Acts 2:42–47)

We can trace all these activities directly back to Jesus' instructions on the Great Commandment as well as his Great Commission. We have "church words" we use now to describe what they were doing: worship, fellowship, discipleship, service, and evangelism. At the end of the day, it doesn't matter what you call them. Their love was action-based and the Church grew—daily!

As I look at this passage and take note of all the things the believers are doing, I notice an underlying theme to it all: sacrifice. This type of living is not about meeting some minimum standard. Words like "devoted," "everything," and "each day" demonstrate a level of commitment and faith much deeper than what simple admiration or rule-following can bring.

Living and loving this way had a profound effect on the community around them. People were attracted to the way of Jesus because people are attracted to sacrificial love. This love created a strong body of unity in the Church as well:

All the believers were united in heart and mind. And they felt that what they owned was not their own, so they shared everything they had. The apostles testified powerfully to the resurrection of the Lord Jesus, and God's great blessing was upon them all. (Acts 4:32–33)

The Church didn't stop at just loving each other sacrificially. They began to reach out around them, and in their community there were plenty of opportunities. Jerusalem, where Jesus was crucified and Christianity first began to grow, was just an outpost in a vast Roman Empire. In Roman culture, life didn't have the same intrinsic value we place on it today. People served the needs of the empire. Therefore, each one's worth was based on their abilities. The sick and infirm, disabled and vulnerable were often cast out of the home to save resources for those who could advance the empire. Female babies and those born with birth defects were often taken to the edge of town to die of exposure. It was a very cruel culture.

Very soon Christians began taking the sick and elderly into their homes to nurse them to health or comfort them in death. They began bringing abandoned children into their families. This was a love that cost something. This was a love that attracted others to join.

Over the centuries, Christians became more organized and built special buildings to take care of the sick on a large scale. You know them today as hospitals. This radical sacrificial love changed the world around them.

So, what keeps us from loving in this way? What keeps us from loving others in a way that costs?

We must break through the barrier of selfishness.

Selfishness doesn't just keep us from following this command of Jesus. Selfishness holds us back from the life that Jesus desires for us, a life that is full and abundant. Selfishness is a barrier to authentic relationships. No relationship can grow without giving of yourself. When we love sacrificially we open our hearts and lives for others to enter. To live selfishly is to live a closed and separated life.

So how do we overcome selfishness? Is it a decision? A simple choice? A prayer we pray for God to remove it from our life?

Yes, it is these . . . and something else. We have another antidote, something we can *do* that counteracts the effects of selfishness in our lives. The antidote to selfishness is generosity.

Every summer my wife and I like to take our kids on a fun family vacation. Because I'm in ministry, my kids get dragged around to a lot of church events and I get pulled away often. We have a very busy schedule, so our vacations are important to us. They are our protected time. We save up and plan all year to create a memorable experience for our family. It doesn't usually cost a lot because we look for deals, camp quite a bit, and drive everywhere.

This past summer, however, we went all out. We planned to go to Washington, D.C., for the Fourth of July. We would spend ten days in the capital—and we bought plane tickets! For the months leading up to the trip we protected the time, we saved up, we prepaid, we made reservations . . . we knew it was going to be awesome.

At the same time we were making all these amazing vacation plans, a couple from our small group was making some amazing plans of their own. They were going to adopt a child. Each week they updated the group on their progress; some weeks were full of frustration while others were hope-filled and encouraging. We prayed for them often and were genuinely excited about their new journey.

If you know anything about adoptions, you probably know that they are very expensive. There are agency fees, lawyers, paperwork, birth mom's care, and in this case travel to another state. The costs were adding up significantly. I would love to say my immediate response was to help them out financially. But it wasn't. I didn't connect their need with an opportunity to help because I was too busy thinking about all the plans I had for the money I set aside. It wasn't until my wife brought up the need that I considered helping.

As soon as the thought to help occurred, another voice piped up in my head. "If you help them, you are going to have to scale something back on your trip." There was not exactly an "extra cash" envelope sitting around our house. If we helped them, it was going to cost us. Selfishness was rearing its ugly head and I was struggling. There was only one way to fight this feeling: I pulled out my checkbook and we wrote a check to help with their adoption. It wasn't a lot, and compared to how much they had to raise, some might call it inconsequential. But it was generous, and that act of generosity was the antidote to my selfish attitude.

Do you know what? We had an amazing vacation. We did everything we wanted. God filled in the gap. God gives us everything we need to be generous. I love how God always does that.

There is another couple from my church who have a similar story. Shaka and Janeen are an amazing couple. Shaka is retired military and Janeen works in local government. After retirement, Shaka started up his own business installing home audio-visual systems. As his business grew, he began making plans for a large garage on his property. It would be used to store his work truck and help the business grow, but, as he admitted, it was also going to be his "man cave."

They had recently completed Dave Ramsey's Financial Peace program at our church and had paid off a lot of debt. So they were saving up for this expense with cash, and getting close to the amount needed to start the project.

As the end of the year neared, our church had a big meeting out in Buckeye, a community to the west of us, where God was leading us to start another campus of Palm Valley Church. As the vision for the expansion was set before those in attendance, Shaka got one of those unmistakable convictions.

Later that night he told his wife that he felt led to give some money to help the campus get started. Not just a little . . . a lot. In fact, he felt like God was asking him to give everything he had saved for the new garage.

He wrote the check and the dream garage was gone.

But God loves generosity.

Within the next few months another house down the street from Shaka and Janeen came on the market. It seemed too good to be true because it was bigger and newer than their current house, but cheaper—and with a giant garage!

When we love sacrificially, we overcome selfishness with generosity in our lives.

Challenge #2

Demonstrate sacrificial love toward someone you know.

The challenge is to love in a way that costs you something. That standard was set by Jesus himself when he gave up everything for us. We are now called to love like he loved: sacrificially.

The first step in this challenge is to identify what would be a sacrifice for you. It's different for everyone. I shared two examples involving a financial gift; that would certainly be a sacrifice to many, but not everyone.

What is something you could do that would be a sacrifice?

You can help someone out by purchasing something they need, paying off a debt, or covering a bill. You could arrange for them to go on a trip or take a much-needed break. You could pay for a nice evening out for a young struggling family. The possibilities are endless.

You could go down the time and service path instead. Go into your child's classroom and help the teacher with paperwork. Babysit without pay. Clean a friend's house or do their yard work. Run errands for someone confined to their home.

There is also the emotional approach. Take a friend in crisis out for coffee and just listen. Spend the afternoon talking with an elderly person.

Now that you are thinking of specifics, which area seemed most appealing to you? Was it financial, service, time, or emotional? You are not allowed to do that one.

You see, it's supposed to be a sacrifice! It is supposed to cost *you* something. What is a sacrifice for one person might be easy for another. Over the years I have run into several church members who, when asked to give some time to a project, ask if they can give some money instead. The opposite is true as well; some people would rather give their time than their money.

Remember, this is supposed to be a challenge. Challenges should be challenging.

The next part of this challenge is identifying to whom you are going to demonstrate love. For this challenge I want it to be someone you already know. Someone in your church family or at work. Someone already in your network of relationships. We will be branching out later, so please do not get ahead.

You might have thought of this person and their need immediately. If so, that's great—get to work. If not, be patient. Prayerfully observe what is happening around you the next few days and see what opportunities come up.

We have many families in our church who are foster parents. They have chosen to open their homes to children in our community in need of a loving family for a short time, a long time, or even a lifetime. It is a big commitment and demonstrates a love that costs. Not everyone is called to be a foster parent, but anyone can help a foster parent. When a foster parent, who is living out sacrificial love every day, receives a sacrificial act of love from someone else, the impact is immediate. Not only does it affect that person, it affects the children as well. Bringing a meal, purchasing needed supplies, or giving the couple a night out are all ways to demonstrate a love that costs to members of our church community.

After you complete the challenge, think about the relationship you have with that person. Generosity breaks down the barriers that selfishness creates between us and others.

Chapter 4

Love Those Different than You

Every generation faces a different battle, whether literal or figurative. My grandfather fought in World War II in the Pacific theater. For several years his life revolved around direct combat against the Japanese. In a battle, it is clear who the enemy is—they are the ones shooting at you. I recognize that this is an oversimplification at some level, but I make this statement to draw the contrast to what was happening during this time back home in the United States.

Away from the actual battles, it is harder to identify the enemy during wartime. During World War II, our government rounded up everyone of Japanese descent living in the United States and sent them to internment camps. The American government feared that otherwise they would aid Japan in its war against the United States. Many of these people were United States citizens. Many of them were born in the U.S. and had never even been to Japan. There was simply a belief that since their heritage was Japanese, they had an overriding loyalty to Japan. This was not based on facts; it was based on fear. This is the power of bias.

Bias takes a group, sets aside their individual characteristics, and assigns all of them the worst traits of a few. We then make judgments and develop feelings about this entire group.

Like I said, every generation faces a battle. My generation grew up with the 9/11 attacks and the aftermath. The events of that day are clear: Islamic terrorists hijacked four planes on September 11, 2001, and flew them on suicide missions to inflict death and damage on our country. What was not clear was the identity of the actual enemy. The terrorists were all from the Middle East. They were all Muslim. They all used their Islamic faith as a justification for their actions. Logically, we know that not every Muslim is a terrorist. Even more broadly, we know that not everyone from the Middle East is a terrorist. However, our fears caused us to lump these people together.

I would like to say I am immune to it, but I am not. When I flew in the months and even years after the 9/11 attacks, I would love to say young men wearing Middle Eastern clothing in the airport didn't stand out to me . . . but they did. I had a bias. I was assigning the actions of a few to an entire population.

Bias is powerful. But relationships do not develop in a culture of bias. It's like removing oxygen from a room and trying to start a fire: the potential is just not there. Bias creates division and it is so difficult to root out. The reason it's so hard to remove is that it is emotional. It's about how we feel.

Bias was definitely present during the time of Jesus as well. Jesus' command to love bridges the divides created by our feelings about other people and other groups.

> One day an expert in religious law stood up to test Jesus by asking him this question: "Teacher, what should I do to inherit eternal life?"

> Jesus replied, "What does the law of Moses say? How do you read it?"

> The man answered, "'You must love the LORD your God with all your heart, all your soul, all your strength, and all your mind.' And, 'Love your neighbor as yourself.'"

"Right!" Jesus told him. "Do this and you will live!"

The man wanted to justify his actions, so he asked Jesus, "And who is my neighbor?" (Luke 10:25–29)

We keep coming back to that same statement over and over again: love your neighbor as yourself. In this interaction with a religious leader, Jesus takes the opportunity to give this familiar command new life.

The religious leaders of the day, whether they were priests, Pharisees, Sadducees, or scribes, all subscribed to a certain set of interpretations of the Jewish Scriptures. The law contained 613 commands that every Jew was expected to follow in order to be right with God. That's a whole lot to remember, and to be honest, most of us have a hard enough time following the first ten.

The group that represented the largest segment of the religious leadership were the Pharisees. They are also the ones we find in conflict with Jesus most often throughout the Gospel accounts. This group was birthed in response to foreign influence on Jewish practices. They viewed themselves as the guardians of Jewish orthodoxy, giving special emphasis to the purity laws found in the Scriptures. To live out the letter of the law was the primary focus of their lives.

But here is where the problem arises. If your life revolves around strict adherence to a set of standards, you must be absolutely certain you are following them correctly. Some of the original commands were not specific enough, so further clarification was required. For example, the fourth (third, for Catholics) commandment states, "Remember to observe the Sabbath day by keeping it holy." That statement is open to numerous interpretations. What does it mean to "keep it holy"? The way I keep it holy might be different than the way you keep it holy. Fortunately, the book of Exodus gives some additional guidance:

> Remember to observe the Sabbath day by keeping it holy. You have six days each week for your ordinary work, but the seventh day is a Sabbath day of rest dedicated to the LORD your God. On that day no one in your household may do any work. This includes you, your sons and daughters, your male and female servants, your livestock, and any foreigners living among you. For in six days the LORD made the heavens, the earth, the sea, and everything in them; but on the seventh day he rested. That is why the LORD blessed the Sabbath day and set it apart as holy. (Exodus 20:8–11)

For the average person this is plenty of information. By "keep it holy," God's intention is for us not to do any work or have anyone else do the work for us. God even points out the fact that he rested on the seventh day of Creation and did not work.

However, if your identity is wrapped up in being the most strict, most devoted, and most religious person in your community or even your nation, you need a little more clarification. For example, what is work? Obviously plowing a field is work and cooking meals is work. But is eating an already prepared meal work? Pushing a cart is definitely work, but what if the cart held a dying person who needed help?

This type of thinking resulted in lists of specific things that were allowed and not allowed. For example, you were allowed to write one letter, but not two. You could move an object around in your house, but not from inside to outside. If an object as already outside, you could move it no more than four cubits. There is a list in the *Mishna* of thirty-nine specific actions forbidden on the Sabbath. The *Mishna* is the compilation of the Jewish oral tradition and is a reflection of many of the traditions practiced by the Pharisees.

The details added to the 613 commands of the Law quickly became unmanageable. In fact, the only people really able to keep up with it all were the religious professionals. If you were a shopkeeper, farmer, or fisherman there was no way you had enough time to follow all these rules perfectly. Interestingly enough, it was a bit too much for the religious leaders as well.

> Then Jesus said to the crowds and to his disciples, "The teachers of religious law and the Pharisees are the official interpreters of the law of Moses. So practice and obey whatever they tell you, but don't follow their example. For they don't practice what they teach. They crush people with unbearable religious demands and never lift a finger to ease the burden." (Matthew 23:1–4)

Remember that Jesus is not getting rid of God's command. He is demonstrating and pointing people to the conditions of the heart that God ultimately desires from us. The Pharisees are following the rules, but it is not affecting their hearts. Jesus calls them out publicly on this, saying, "What sorrow awaits you teachers of religious law and you Pharisees. Hypocrites! For you are like whitewashed tombs—beautiful on the outside but filled on the inside with dead people's bones and all sorts of impurity" (Matthew 23:27).

Now, let's go back to the discussion between Jesus and the religious leader about the command to "love your neighbor as yourself." After all this background information on the Pharisees, it probably makes a little more sense that the expert in religious law asked Jesus a follow-up question:

"And who is my neighbor?" "Neighbor" is too general a term. The religious lawyer wants to know specifically to whom he needs to show love. He is worried about following the strict letter of the law, not about the condition of his heart.

Jesus, knowing exactly what was going on in this man's heart, told a story. Jesus was a master storyteller. His parables were crafted specifically to illustrate truths. They are memorable; you only have to hear them once and they can typically be retold with accuracy. These parables spread like wildfire throughout the region as people took the stories home with them. The stories also created tension. Jesus repeatedly addressed extreme examples and sensitive subjects. One can see all of this displayed in his well-known parable of the good Samaritan.

"A Jewish man was traveling from Jerusalem down to Jericho, and he was attacked by bandits. They stripped him of his clothes, beat him up, and left him half dead beside the road.

"By chance a priest came along. But when he saw the man lying there, he crossed to the other side of the road and passed him by. A Temple assistant walked over and looked at him lying there, but he also passed by on the other side." (Luke 10:30–32)

Let's pause here a second. Remember who Jesus is talking to: a religious leader. This is what I like to refer to as "poking the bear." The standard Jewish interpretation of "neighbor" was a fellow Jew. The priest is a Jew, the Temple worker is a Jew, the injured man is a Jew; they are all neighbors. This should be a very short and somewhat boring story of two men doing what any reasonable person would do in their place. But this story is anything but that.

A Jewish man is lying, bleeding and dying, by the side of the road, and two religious leaders cross to the other side to avoid getting too close to him. This act flies in the face of what one would reasonably expect to happen in this situation. Why in the world would they do this? Because of their religious purity laws. If the poor man actually died, which by all accounts seemed highly likely, the priest and the assistant would be unclean for a full week because they touched a dead body. (This is the most forgiving excuse. It also could have just been because they didn't want to be bothered or inconvenienced.)

> "Then a despised Samaritan came along, and when he saw the man, he felt compassion for him." (Luke 10:33)

Who is a Samaritan? Why was the Samaritan so despised? Well, the short answer is that in this time period all Samaritans were despised by the Jews.

The two things that cause division in the world more than anything else are religion and race. Wars have been fought on the basis of religious conviction. Genocides have been committed in attempts to eliminate entire races of people. The Jewish and Samaritan divide touches both of these hot-button issues, and the divide runs deep.

Hundreds of years earlier the Assyrian empire invaded the northern ten tribes of Israel, conquering them and taking the majority of the people away as captives. A remnant group of these tribes was left in the desolated land called Samaria. The Assyrian King Sargon resettled the land with people groups from Babylon, Cuthah, Avva, Hamath, and Sepharvaim. (Don't worry, you won't have to remember those names.) These peoples intermarried with the remaining Israelites, creating an ethnic group distinctly different from the two tribes that made up the southern area, Judah, the "pure Jews." The

Samaritans also combined the religious beliefs of all the groups and ended up with a distorted version of Judaism. They set up their own temple and system for worship.

Both groups claimed to be right. Both groups claimed to be the real chosen people of God. Both groups hated each other. They would avoid each other at all costs. Jews would travel miles out of the way to avoid stepping foot on Samaritan soil.

I bet they were the punchlines of each other's jokes too.

Samaritans were also probably the villains in every Jewish story. So when Jesus made the Samaritan the hero, everyone paid attention.

> "Going over to him, the Samaritan soothed his wounds with olive oil and wine and bandaged them. Then he put the man on his own donkey and took him to an inn, where he took care of him. The next day he handed the innkeeper two silver coins, telling him, 'Take care of this man. If his bill runs higher than this, I'll pay you the next time I'm here.'" (Luke 10:34–35)

If the Samaritan had only given the poor man a drink of water, the crowd would have walked away shocked, but Jesus lays it on thick. The Samaritan goes so far above what would be expected. There were probably some people in the crowd who wouldn't do that much for their actual brother. Yet this despised Samaritan exhibited an exorbitant amount of compassion.

Let's watch Jesus land this plane. He now has a question for the religious leader.

> "Now which of these three would you say was a neighbor to the man who was attacked by bandits?" Jesus asked.

The man replied, "The one who showed him mercy."

Then Jesus said, "Yes, now go and do the same."

(Luke 10:36–37)

By the way, Jesus never directly answered his initial question. The question posed was, "who is my neighbor?" The religious leader wanted to know what was required of him in order to fulfill the law. Essentially, he wanted to know how far his love had to extend to be just enough. It was a question designed to limit and contain the boundaries of his requirement to love.

In the story the injured Jewish man discovered who his neighbor was: the Samaritan who showed him mercy. The Samaritan was the Jew's neighbor. Where the religious leader was trying to minimize his responsibility to love others, Jesus opened the boundaries as far as he could.

Love *the Samaritan* as you love yourself.
Love *someone who speaks differently* as you love
yourself.
Love *someone who looks different* as you love yourself.
Love *someone who was raised differently* as you love
yourself.
Love *someone who lives differently* as you love yourself.
Love *someone who believes differently* as you love
yourself.
Love *someone who worships differently* as you love
yourself.

Just to be clear, I am still talking about the Samaritan . . . or have we moved on to something bigger?

I think what Jesus was telling us in this parable is that we don't get to exclude certain types or groups of people from love.

Our bias limits the extent to which we are willing to love others.

I recently watched a documentary about one of my heroes, Fred Rogers. It was called *Won't You Be My Neighbor?*. Now before you email me telling me he was a sniper or always wore sweaters because of his tattoos, save your time and watch the movie.

For those of you who don't know, Fred Rogers had a show for children that ran on public television in the United States for over thirty years called *Mister Rogers' Neighborhood*. He was one of those rare TV personalities whose show aligned with his convictions, which in turn aligned with his personal life. Children's television was not a career for him; it was his mission. In fact, it was more of a calling. Fred Rogers was an ordained minister. Upon completing seminary he was ordained with the commission to minister to children through the medium of television. That's a pretty specific charge, but one given by someone who understood Rogers' specific gifts and abilities. Throughout his show he took the command to love your neighbor and wove it into every episode.

And he didn't mind addressing the biases of the day. Mr. Rogers started his program during the late 1960s, as the civil rights movement in the United States was in full swing. He never preached to or lectured children. In fact, if you were a parent, you might miss some of the subtle ways he broke down the barriers of bias. To project a positive image for children he cast an African American gentleman as the neighborhood's police officer. This was not a minor character, but a prominent recurring role. Mr. Rogers knew there were many young black children looking for a positive role model on television, and he gave that to them.

And then there were the not-so-subtle scenes. There is a famous series of photos from 1964 that records a hotel manager pouring bleach on a group of African American students swimming in the pool at his hotel. It was common in the south at that time to have segregated facilities for black people and white people: bathrooms, drinking fountains, dining areas, and swimming pools. Fred Rogers found it ridiculous and could not believe that little children were being exposed to these ideas and had seen these horrible images. What could he do?

It's another beautiful day in the neighborhood as the camera focuses on Mr. Rogers sitting in a chair with his feet in an ankle-deep children's play pool. There is talk of the hot weather and the cool water. It's Mr. Rogers, doing what he does best, talking to kids at their level about normal everyday things. And then in walks Officer Clemmons, the African American police officer. Of course, Mr. Rogers immediately invited him to pull up a chair and cool off his feet with him. The average child watching at home didn't bat an eye. If Mr. Rogers and Officer Clemmons want to take a swim together, then it must be okay. Parents watching in the background might have felt a little more apprehension. They were probably wondering, how far is he going to take this?

Just a little bit further.

Officer Clemmons didn't bring a towel to dry off with, but don't worry, Mr. Rogers offers to share his. In fact, he just dries off Officer Clemmons' feet himself, all while smiling gently at the camera.

Whom do we love? Everyone. There is no place for bias is Mr. Rogers' neighborhood . . . or in the kingdom of God.

The parable of the Good Samaritan centers on an extreme act of compassion. His emotional response to the suffering he witnessed led the Samaritan to take immediate action. Jesus has this same type of response. Throughout the

Gospels we hear that Jesus, moved by compassion, began healing the sick.

Compassion looks beyond the circumstances to the suffering. It didn't matter where the injured man was from—all the Good Samaritan focused on was his suffering.

Are you able to see suffering beyond your biases?

It's easy to demonstrate love to your friends and people who can return the favor. Everyone does that. What is special is when you demonstrate love to someone different than you.

I have two incredible friends named Pat and Fritz. There are a couple of things about these guys that make our relationship unique; one is that they are Catholic and I am a pastor of a Protestant church. I can tell you that there are very few people I know who love Jesus more than these two men and even fewer who have given more of themselves to serve him. I think that's why we get along so well.

Pat and Fritz are members of the Focolare. It's a movement started in northern Italy during World War II. As the local towns and villages were bombed because of the Nazi occupation, Chiara Lubich and a few close friends would pass the time in the air raid shelters reading a small copy of the New Testament and then committing to go out and do whatever it said to do in their community. The words of Jesus and his commands to love became the primary focus of their lives in this incredibly difficult and frightening time.

At the end of the war they continued the practices of studying Scripture, prayer, and service toward others through concrete acts of love, and the group grew in size. Communities began to form with the express purpose of living out the commands of Jesus to love and encouraging others to do so. Pat and Fritz both have incredible accounts of personal encounters with Christ that led them to join this community and serve God with their whole lives.

The patron saint of the Focolare Movement is Mary, the mother of God. I didn't know this for quite some time after I met Pat and Fritz, and honestly I am glad that I didn't. As a Baptist pastor, too much focus on the Virgin Mary makes me uncomfortable. I know it would have changed my first impressions of the guys. Instead, I just saw them and got to know them through the lens of their actions, speech, and hearts.

Eventually, I discovered the Focolare's emphasis on Mary, and by then it was easy to have a conversation about it. I was honestly just confused. Why all the focus on her? It seemed to me that all they ever talked about was Jesus. Why isn't Jesus their "patron saint"?

The answer made complete sense . . . even to my non-Catholic, Baptist-trained mind. My friend Pat took me to Scripture and began to unpack the ministry of Mary.

First of all, Mary was a servant of God whom he used to bring Jesus into the world. The next passage Pat pointed me to was Jesus' first miracle, where Mary asked him to save the party because they ran out of wine. Mary's instructions to the servants were very simple: "Do whatever he tells you" (John 2:5). And finally, Pat asked where Mary was the rest of Jesus' ministry. She was most likely there all the time. The group of women who traveled with the disciples supporting Jesus' ministry most likely included his mother. Yet we don't find her up front.

"That's why Mary is our example," Pat concluded. "Our mission is to take Jesus to the world and encourage people to do whatever he says. We do this by staying in the background and serving Jesus."

That makes a lot of sense and, to my relief, is not weird at all.

Pointing people to do what Jesus told us to do. I understand that completely. In fact, that is what this book is all about.

I definitely had some bias toward Catholics. My relationship with Pat and Fritz broke down that barrier as compassion toward each other broke down the bias. Within the relationship we found the safe space to have conversations about our differences and come to an understanding that was deep and enriching.

When we love those different than us, we overcome bias with compassion.

Challenge #3

Demonstrate love to someone different than you.

The easy part of this challenge is finding someone different than us. We are pretty good at that. We naturally create categories that separate people, whether by race, culture, religion, economic status, political affiliation, education, career choice, or even their hobbies or sports allegiances.

Those are the big buckets; we can divide these down even further. We could take education and made big distinctions about the levels of education: GED, high school diploma, trade certifications, bachelor's degree, master's degree, doctorate. We could talk about public versus private education or even the type of science you studied (because everyone knows physicists are superior to biologists).

For this challenge I want you to think of a group that goes beyond just being different. I want you to pick one you actively have a bias against. The kind of bias that makes you really not want to do anything nice for them. Not because of something they have done to you specifically—that would make them an enemy, and we are still working up to that.

It could be a department at your work that you are rivals with. Or it could be a member of the political party that you are not a part of. Maybe it is a group of neighbors whose lifestyle is completely different than your own.

Now, wait for them to need help . . . and help them.

You probably don't even need to wait. There are people in need of help all around you. The reason you don't notice them is because you probably have your bias-blinders on. Ask God to help you see the needs and suffering of those around you regardless of who they are.

Chapter 5

Love the Difficult

Over the past several years I have spent quite a bit of time in the African nation of Côte d'Ivoire, or the Ivory Coast. Our church partners with Rick Warren's initiative to Africa that focuses on helping healthy local churches become difference makers in their community. The key to the initiative is building unity in the Christian Church so that together believers can transform each nation. It's a pretty big project. It's a God-sized project.

My church has adopted Côte d'Ivoire for the initiative. This means that several times a year I meet with local Ivorian leaders to work on three things.

First up is the training. We develop training methods, programs, and coaching networks in order to equip pastors in a balanced approach to ministry. This approach guides the pastor in intentionally developing church members to become fully devoted followers of Jesus who are compelled to live out their faith in the community where they live.

The second thing I work on is gathering a team of nationally recognized Ivorian leaders to bring unity to the movement. We call it our steering team. Right now, it consists of the denominational heads of the Baptists, Methodists, Assembly of God, Christian Missionary Alliance, Church of Pentecost, and Church of Pentecost Côte d'Ivoire, along with presidents of three national Evangelical federations representing tens of thousands of local churches, and a handful of influential mega church pastors and evangelists. It's quite the group.

The third component is to guide the steering team to weigh in on the biggest needs of the country. We look at the country's spiritual issues, corruption problems, economic challenges, health crises, and gaps in education. Through prayer and the guidance of the Holy Spirit these godly leaders have come together in agreement in order to focus on specific initiatives as an entire group. There is power in unified efforts like these.

I am completely unqualified to lead an initiative of this magnitude and influence. I don't have the experience. I don't have the expertise. I don't have the resources. Fortunately, those are not the things this effort needs the most. What makes all this work is the Holy Spirit's work through relationships. It's really all about relationships, and authentic relationships are all about love.

Some of my closest friends in ministry are from Côte d'Ivoire. We have prayed together and cried together. These are real deep relationships that are felt even when we are thousands of miles apart. But it took time. In fact, if I had to boil down the love language of this culture, I would say it is time. There is a saying that my friend Marc tells me: "You Americans have watches, but we have the time."

The greatest gains made in this project so far did not happen in a classroom or one of our big conferences. They happened sitting around tables sharing meals. Long meals. Long conversations. Long trips. Since the initiative began, I have averaged about a month of time each year in Côte d'Ivoire.

Although it is difficult to travel so far and it's very difficult to be away from my family and church for so long, these relationships have been easy to build, because the people I have met are easy to love. We have so much in common: our faith, our ministry struggles, our family dynamics. We never run out of things to talk about. It's easy to love people like that!

Jesus' command to love goes beyond loving the lovable, however, and it was in Côte d'Ivoire where I learned this lesson too.

Rose has been a key member of the team in Côte d'Ivoire since we first started working there. She was a ministry leader in a local church in Abidjan (the country's largest city, with almost five million people) and is blessed with the gifts of administration—and getting things done. Her full-time job was running the communications department of the major hospital in Abidjan. Every time we would arrive in country, she would take leave from her job to assist our efforts.

I had always heard about her job from others and knew she was a pretty big deal. However, I never fully understood it until she took us to her office one afternoon after we insisted we see where she worked. As we toured the administrative offices she beamed as she introduced us to her colleagues. After a while we made our way back to her office and sat down for a cup of the coffee her interns had prepared while we were out.

As we drank coffee, we asked more about the hospital, the challenges of healthcare in Côte d'Ivoire, and the stress of being a working parent (Rose had recently had a baby). Eventually, the conversation moved to one of the areas of the hospital that Rose was most proud of, the burn clinic. Her hospital has one of the most extensive burn clinics in West Africa. Patients are brought here from surrounding countries to be treated for months at a time as their burns heal.

"Would you like a tour?" Rose asked excitedly.

"Absolutely not," I immediately thought, but fortunately I did not vocalize it.

As a pastor I am called to make hospital visits quite a lot. Most of the time it's not a big deal. I pray with members of our church before surgeries. I visit people who are ill, sometimes at death's door. This stuff doesn't bother me at all, and I count it a privilege to minister in this way. The average hospital visit in the United States does not involve staring at open wounds.

But the thought of a burn unit terrified me. When Adrienne was in nursing school, she had to do a clinical rotation on a burn unit. She told me about the processes required to bring health back to badly burned areas. It involved removing dead skin daily, and the patient was in excruciating pain. I didn't know a lot about burn units (because I made her stop talking), but I knew enough to know I did not want to be in one.

"Would you like a tour?" Rose asked again.

This time I found myself speaking words that my mind did not agree with. "Of course, I would love to take a tour."

The walk over to the clinic from the administrative offices gave me just enough time to really get my mind racing. Thoughts of the pain and the injuries I would soon be exposed to caused my anxiety to build with each step. I didn't think I would be able to do it.

As we arrived at the clinic, we were ushered into the resident doctor's office. Assistants and nurses were buzzing around excitedly. I wasn't sure if the energy filling the room was because of Rose's presence or ours. Regardless of who caused the excitement, it was apparent that tours were not a common occurrence at the burn clinic.

A medical worker assisted us in putting on sterile gowns as the doctor told us about the clinic. I didn't hear a word he said. We were then led out of the office into the inner courtyard of the clinic. I was immediately overwhelmed. There were sounds of crying and there were people everywhere leaning up against the walls and laying on mats in the shade. These were local burn victims, with hands, legs, faces turned ugly shades of red from the burns. We were told that these were the relatively mild cases and that they came in daily for their wound care. The severely burned patients were inside. They did not get to go to their homes at night; many of them would be here for weeks and even months recovering from their injuries.

As we walked in the first room I was immediately taken aback by the sights, sounds, and smells. The stifling African heat and humidity were present even in this medical environment. The only relief came from fans placed throughout the long open room, which contained five or six patients. The smell is what caught me by surprise. I was so preoccupied by what I was afraid to see, I never gave any thought to what my nose would encounter. Shallow mouth breathing was my coping skill. And then there were the burns themselves. The majority of the patients' bodies were covered by severe burns which had removed layer upon layer of skin. It was shockingly quieter in this room; no loud cries, just occasional low groans as people slowly moved around in their beds to find a comfortable position to rest. This quieter environment was most likely due to the availability of pain medication in the in-patient unit.

I stood there taking it all in. The translator was saying something in the background but I couldn't hear her. I wanted to run out. I wanted to shut my eyes. It was too difficult for me.

But then I caught the eyes of one of the patients as they stared at me, this American pastor who was seeing them at one of the most vulnerable times of their life. For a moment I didn't notice the burns or sounds or smells, I just saw a young man. As I slowly stepped forward, I asked myself, "What can I do for this man? I can't relieve his pain or heal his burns. He's already getting the best care available to him." But I felt like I just needed to get closer.

As I approached the bed, I lifted up my hand, feeling like I wanted to touch him, but not finding a safe place to put it, I raised it up as a greeting. I spoke quietly in a language he probably didn't understand, and I prayed for him. That was it. I couldn't give him much, but I gave him my presence. I did this several times throughout the tour, stopping and praying, getting close to the victims. God helped me to see a fellow person made in the image of God through the pain, suffering, and trauma.

I learned a very important lesson that day about love. The situations that make me feel the most uncomfortable do so because I feel out of control. The reason I feel this way is because of my own limitations, whether actual or imagined. When I cannot fix someone's problems, it is much easier to stay away and avoid the situation completely. What I learned in the burn unit was that I don't have to fix anything or solve anyone's problem to show love. My presence alone was a demonstration of love. It is not easy; in fact it was one of the most difficult things I have ever done.

Jesus' command to love others is not limited to those who are easy for us to love.

Halfway through my doctorate program, when I had finished all my coursework, there was a series of comprehensive exams on every core class we had taken up to this point: material physics, phase transformations, thermodynamics, and quantum physics. The good news was that if you received an A in a class, you didn't need to take that comprehensive exam. The bad news was that I had to take all the comprehensive exams.

I spent a full semester preparing for the exams. It was all I thought about. If I did not pass these tests, I would not be allowed to move on in my studies and finish my Ph.D. research. The pressure was the most I had ever felt. I even grew a beard . . . before they were cool.

We have all had pressure-packed moments in life—a test or exam, a certification, an interview, your first big work project. These are "make it or break it" moments. To succeed means to advance in your education or career. To fail means a major setback or even the loss of an opportunity.

I don't like being judged like this, and you probably don't either. It would be much fairer if someone was able to look at our entire body of work over a long period of time in order to judge our abilities. How can an hour-long exam reflect what I really know? What if I was just having a bad day? What if I am just bad at taking tests? The system didn't seem very fair.

God has a perfect sense of justice, so one can assume there is no comprehensive exam when we finally meet him face to face. But that is not to say there is no judgment.

Let me take a moment to summarize some very important thoughts about God's judgment.

God is perfect and holy and cannot sin; in fact he cannot even associate with sin. When mankind rebelled against God by stepping out of his boundaries and disobeying his commands it caused an immediate separation between God and man. To be clear: man walked away from God; God did not walk away from man. In order for human beings to be back in a relationship with God, the sin in our lives that separates us from God needed to be removed. The only way for this to happen was for God to come down himself and give up his life as a sacrifice for our sins.

So how do we ourselves obtain that forgiveness? Many people think that we must earn it. If I do good deeds, pray, read the Bible, serve others, or give my money I can somehow earn the forgiveness Jesus paid for on the cross. The problem with that plan is this: how good is good enough? How much do I have to do to earn God's forgiveness? With a system like that we would live in constant fear and insecurity, not knowing our status with God.

The forgiveness that we so desperately desire is actually a grace given to us by God. Grace is an undeserved, unearned, free gift. Our relationship with God is not dependent on what *we* do, it's based on what *he* did and the grace he offers us.

Even with all that being said, what we choose to do in this life still matters. There will be a final judgment, not a quiz or exam, but a full review of one's life. Those who have received the gift of grace from God will be brought into his presence and rewarded for their action, and those who have chosen to reject God's grace will be eternally separated from God's presence.

A complete review of my life. That's pretty daunting. When I think of my life so far, I can say there will probably be more negative highlights than positive. My acts of disobedience, my internal thoughts, and missed opportunities to serve are what worry me most. But there will also probably be some positive surprises—at least I hope so! In fact, Jesus explains why we might experience some unexpected blessings as he describes to his disciples and followers what the final judgment will look like.

> "Then the King will say to those on his right, 'Come, you who are blessed by my Father, inherit the Kingdom prepared for you from the creation of the world. For I was hungry, and you fed me. I was thirsty, and you gave me a drink. I was a stranger, and you invited me into your home. I was naked, and you gave me clothing. I

was sick, and you cared for me. I was in prison, and you visited me.'

"Then these righteous ones will reply, 'Lord, when did we ever see you hungry and feed you? Or thirsty and give you something to drink? Or a stranger and show you hospitality? Or naked and give you clothing? When did we ever see you sick or in prison and visit you?'

"And the King will say, 'I tell you the truth, when you did it to one of the least of these my brothers and sisters, you were doing it to me!'" (Matthew 25:34–40)

In this passage Jesus highlights simple acts of love that meet the needs of people: clothing, food, water, shelter, presence. There is nothing overly generous about these acts in themselves. In fact, they are the very basic necessities for survival. When it comes down to it, we don't need a lot to survive. However, we often confuse our wants with our needs.

We want a three-bedroom house for our family, but what we need is shelter.

We want an ice-cold soda to drink, but we need a cup of water.

We want a designer jacket, but we need a coat to keep us warm.

We want a feast at every meal, but we need a bowl of food.

We want to be the center of the party, but we need one authentic friend.

The acts of love Jesus presented were simple and basic. In fact, they are overly simple so as not to distract from the point he is making. The focus of the passage is not on what act of love they showed, but for whom they did it: "the least of these."

Jesus directs us to the most vulnerable and least-thought-of people in our culture: the homeless, the needy, the sick, the criminals, and the foreigners. Do you know what else these groups all have in common? They are difficult to love. Each one has its own complication. Each one comes with its own reason why it is easier to just ignore the problem.

Then Jesus makes this amazing connection between serving him and serving "the least of these": he says it's the same thing. "*When you did it to one of the least of these my brothers and sisters, you were doing it to me.*" He didn't say it was *like* you were doing it to me. He said you *were* doing it to me. In some mysterious supernatural way, we are actually serving Jesus himself.

Mother Teresa of Calcutta committed her life to the least of these. To read her biography is to view a life lived with a single purpose. As a young nun serving in India she was moved by the needs of the outcasts and poor. Crushing poverty led to the sick, dying, and deformed being cast into the streets like trash. This young nun began to step into the hopeless situation one person at a time. She was eventually given permission to begin her own order, the Missionaries of Charity, which now has members throughout the world.

According to Fr. Brian Kolodiejchuk, the editor of *Come Be My Light: The Private Writings of the Saint of Calcutta*, Mother Teresa would often summarize her mission as the "Gospel on five fingers." You-did-it-to-me: one word for each finger.

Loving the unlovable was directly connected to her love for Jesus. This was not a non-profit charity or an aid organization. This was a group of Jesus' followers doing what he commanded them to do. For this reason, Jesus had to remain central to their work lives. Without full dependence on him, the whole effort was helpless. Mother Teresa and her co-workers adhered to a disciplined regimen of worship, prayer, and reflection to foster a reliance on God and to keep him central in their work. Kathryn Spink, in her biography of Mother Teresa, shares a story about how adamant she was about this. At one point a group of brothers were running a leper colony in relationship with the Missionaries of Charity. The work was hard and overwhelming. After a while the time required to meet the needs of the lepers began to take away from the brothers' private devotional time. Mother Teresa's instructions were simple: "Tell your brothers, if they do not want to be holy, they can go home."

So what is it that keeps us from reaching out to those who are difficult to love? I believe it is fear. We are afraid of situations we cannot control. We are afraid of problems we cannot easily fix. We are afraid of weird or uncomfortable situations that might come up. We are afraid of not having the right answers.

As I walked into the burn clinic in Abidjan I was full of fear. But as God helped me look beyond everything I was afraid of, I saw people created in God's image who needed my presence. I couldn't offer anything else to them that day other than being with them. Being present drove out my fear. I can honestly say that if I were asked to go back to the burn unit, I wouldn't have an issue with it. I don't have the same fear I had before—it's gone.

You probably won't be able to fix all the problems of the people you encounter with your act of love, but by being present we can bridge a gap that should not exist between two people created in God's image. When we love the difficult to love we overcome fear with presence.

Challenge #4

Love someone difficult to love.

It is impossible to completely solve a person's problems in one encounter. This is never more apparent than when we encounter who Jesus referred to as "the least of these." They are not the least of these because they are any less valuable; they are the least of these because they are often forgotten.

You can give a homeless person a meal or something to drink and several hours later they will be hungry and thirsty again. Any gift of clothing will eventually wear out. The prisoner will still be in prison, the sick will still be bedridden. All of this screams, stay away, you are wasting your time!

That is why the challenge is to get close.

Some situations make us nervous. I am not talking about being scared for your safety—I'm talking about being around people who are really struggling: people who are homeless, people with mental illness, prisoners, the sick, and the dying.

You may or may not assist them with a physical need. But you must engage them personally. The act of love is your presence.

When was the last time this person got a handshake, a loving hand on the shoulder, a warm hug?

When was the last time they had a conversation and were asked about themselves?

Presence drives out fear.

There is a woman who attends my church who did something surprising last Christmas. I say it was surprising because she surprised herself. As she was headed into Walmart during the busyness of Christmas shopping, she noticed a homeless man sitting outside. Her immediate emotions of fear and nervousness were overcome by a nudge from God to reach out to the man. She veered over in his direction and asked him if he needed any help and he indicated that he was hungry and could use a bite to eat. "Whew!" she thought. "I can do that."

While in the store doing her shopping, she grabbed some food and drink for the man and was looking forward to dropping it off with him on her way back to her car. But as she approached him, she felt the need to talk to him, and not just drop off the food. This is not normal for her. She isn't naturally extraverted. She doesn't strike up conversations with strangers. She definitely does not strike up conversations with homeless men. But the next thing she knew she was talking to this man and sharing God's love with him. Not preaching at him, but letting him know how much God loved him and how much she loved him. As she told me this story the next week, she was still amazed at the words that had come out of her mouth. God was definitely speaking encouragement through her to the man. The entire encounter left her changed. It wasn't the food that made a difference, it was her presence. God removed her fear as she stepped in and offered her presence to this man created in God's image. That day she served Jesus.

You are going to have to go outside your current relationships for this challenge. You are going to have to seek this encounter out. But it's not going to be hard. The "least of these," the people who are difficult to love, are everywhere. It might involve you refocusing your efforts because over time we tend to tune these people out.

As you step into the encounter, wait for the miracle to happen. No, not a miracle that changes their situation. The miracle that happens when you find that you are actually loving Jesus.

Chapter 6

Love Your Enemy

Jim Elliot was an American missionary to Ecuador during the 1950s. He and his wife, Elisabeth, committed their lives to sharing the love of Christ with those who have never heard it. The only proper motive for mission work is love, and the Elliots and their friends demonstrated this in a very incredible way.

In 1956, Jim, along with four other missionaries, Pete Fleming, Nate Saint, Ed McCully, and Roger Youderian, began making contact with an unreached tribe in remote Ecuador called the Aucas. This tribe had a reputation for violence and was already known to have murdered several Shell Oil Company workers who had previously made contact. The missionaries spent several months working to build a rapport with the group by dropping gifts from their small plane and eventually setting up a shelter outside the Aucas village to make daily contact and hopefully build a relationship. The missionaries believed the violence of this tribe could only change by the power of God.

After several friendly encounters and some positive progress, the Aucas suddenly murdered all five missionaries by spear. As word of the violence made its way around the world people were shocked. However, this shock was nothing compared to what would happen next.

Two years later, Elisabeth Elliot and Rachel Saint, Nate Saint's sister, traveled to the Aucas tribe. They did not go for closure or justice; they went for love. They moved into the village and learned the Aucas' culture and language. They came and forgave the people who murdered their loved ones.

This act of forgiveness so moved the Waodani people, as they are now called, that they were ready to hear about God's love for them and the forgiveness that Jesus offers.

The women's forgiveness and their relationship with the people were so authentic that years later Nate Saint's son, Steve, moved his family from Florida to live with the Waodani people. His children refer to the tribal elder who killed their grandfather as "Grandfather."

We hear stories about this type of forgiveness, and it moves us. There is something inside us that resonates with the ability to forgive such terrible acts. Yet, to actually forgive that way, to show love to our enemies, is incredibly difficult. That's why we have saved this challenge for last.

Jesus' teaching about the kingdom of heaven stirred up quite the controversy. Every time he began teaching with the phrase, "you have heard the law that says . . ." the Pharisees and religious leaders took the remark personally. You see, they were the ones saying that stuff. It was their responsibility to instruct the people in the commands of God and to teach the public how to live rightly.

The average person could not read or write at this time. Even if they could, they probably could not read ancient Hebrew, the language in which the Scriptures were written. And if they could read ancient Hebrew, there were very few copies of the Scriptures available. The copies were protected and stored in the Temple and local synagogues. The only way to know what the Scriptures said was to go to the Temple or synagogue on the Sabbath and listen to the religious leaders read and explain how to live it out. Then you would go home that day having "heard the law that says."

Every time Jesus taught, he challenged the interpretation and emphasis the Pharisees and other religious leaders placed on the Jewish Law.

The people loved it.

The religious elite hated it.

Over the course of history, many people who challenge the status quo, specifically in the area of religion, don't end up living very long. It is this conflict between Jesus and the religious leaders that eventually led to his crucifixion.

Jesus taught this way—upending long-held interpretations—because the previous way of thinking had led to ritualistic religion. When God gave these commands and instructions in the first place, the purpose was to affect the people's hearts and set them apart as a special people. God was using the commands to bring about his plan of redemption. It was a simple covenant, relationship: If you follow my commands, then you will receive my blessing.

What Jesus was doing was setting the terms for a New Covenant. The old agreement was completed with his death, and the New Covenant, the reality of the kingdom of heaven, became available to all.

The prophet Jeremiah made reference to this fulfillment hundreds of years earlier.

> "The day is coming," says the Lord, "when I will make a new covenant with the people of Israel and Judah. This covenant will not be like the one I made with their ancestors when I took them by the hand and brought them out of the land of Egypt. They broke that covenant, though I loved them as a husband loves his wife," says the Lord.

> "But this is the new covenant I will make with the people of Israel after those days," says the Lord. "I

will put my instructions deep within them, and
I will write them on their hearts. I will be their
God, and they will be my people. And they will
not need to teach their neighbors, nor will they
need to teach their relatives, saying, 'You should
know the Lord.' For everyone, from the least
to the greatest, will know me already," says the
Lord. "And I will forgive their wickedness, and I
will never again remember their sins." (Jeremiah
31:31–34)

It is an agreement written on our hearts. There will no
longer be a religious elite class as the gatekeepers, because
everyone can know God.

Every time Jesus taught, the divide between himself
and the religious leaders grew larger and larger. The people
sided with Jesus. That didn't mean they always understood
what he taught. And it certainly didn't mean they understood all the implications of the New Covenant he was
establishing. But they loved him. They wanted to follow his
teaching—for the most part. There were times when people
walked away because the path Jesus set before them was too
difficult. There were other times when they were just confused. When Jesus got to this particular teaching, everyone
was left scratching their heads.

"You have heard the law that says the punishment
must match the injury: 'An eye for an eye, and a
tooth for a tooth.' But I say, do not resist an evil
person! If someone slaps you on the right cheek,
offer the other cheek also. If you are sued in court
and your shirt is taken from you, give your coat,
too. If a soldier demands that you carry his gear
for a mile, carry it two miles. Give to those who
ask, and don't turn away from those who want to
borrow." (Matthew 5:38–42)

This cannot be right, you might think—and many of the people who heard Jesus agreed. If someone actually lived like this, they would be a doormat for everyone to walk over. No self-respecting person could live this way for very long; everyone has their limits.

This reminds me of a famous Kenny Rogers song called "Coward of the County." As the song goes, Tommy was just ten years old when his father died in prison. His father's final words to his young son are the chorus of the song:

> Promise me, son, not to do the things I've done
> Walk away from trouble if you can
> It won't mean you're weak if you turn the other cheek
> I hope you're old enough to understand
> Son, you don't have to fight to be a man

Tommy takes his father's dying words to heart and never gets into a fight growing up. For this he is labeled a coward by the entire town and is often taken advantage of. That is, until some guys mess with his girlfriend, and he beats them up. There are a few more details . . . but you can listen to the song yourself.

In the final chorus, the last line is changed to: "Sometimes you gotta fight when you're a man." When that line echoes through bars and saloons around the wild Southwest where I am from, I imagine beer bottles being broken and cheers rising up from the crowd, because that's the type of ending that we celebrate. Tommy finally got tired of turning the other cheek and those men got what was coming to them.

How many books and movies carry this same theme? You probably don't have to think hard to name a few. Vengeance stories are made into blockbuster movies and novels all the time because the storyline makes us feel good. It satisfies our own personal sense of justice.

Jesus says, no, not in my kingdom.

But in the kingdom the Jewish people were living in, this would be hard to live out. They were under Roman occupation at this time. That whole statement about a soldier forcing you to go one mile was a direct reference to the Roman soldiers who could at any time conscript people to carry their gear or deliver messages or materials. Jesus says to not only carry the load, but carry it twice as far as required.

Why would they ever do something like that for the people who oppress and tax them? Why would they do this for the rulers who sometimes acted with utter cruelty? Several decades earlier, the Roman general Publius Quinctilius Varus intervened in a Jewish revolt. At the end of the day the towns of Sepphoris and Emmaus were completely destroyed and two thousand Jewish rebels were publicly crucified for all to see what happens to those who cause problems for Rome.

Yes, help those guys.

And Jesus was not done yet.

"You have heard the law that says, 'Love your neighbor and hate your enemy.' But I say, love your enemies! Pray for those who persecute you! In that way, you will be acting as true children of your Father in heaven." (Matthew 5:43–45)

I can only imagine the questions Jesus received: "So not only am I not to seek revenge, I am also supposed to show love to my enemies? And seeing that you brought up the Romans, I don't suppose they might be included in this list of enemies I am supposed to love, would they?"

Yes, the Romans would be included on the list to love as well.

Who could possibly show this kind of love? Who could set aside all the wrongs committed against them and not only forgo vengeance, but actively demonstrate love toward that person?

It's like asking a family member of a 9/11 victim to donate money to the families of the hijackers.

It's like asking the wife of a man who was lynched to bake a cake for the next KKK rally.

Who does that type of thing? Who waives retribution and opts for love?

God does.

Jesus came to earth to do just that.

Jesus also told a story about what God is like to make sure we really understood it. It went something like this:

There once was a man who was very wealthy and had two sons. The younger son did not like living under his father's rules and authority. He believed life would be better for him if he could set out on his own. So, he went to his father to ask for his inheritance early. This was a highly unusual request; in fact, it was quite insulting. Essentially the young son was telling his father that he couldn't wait for him to die and he wanted his father's money now. What was even more unusual than the request was the father's agreement to pay it out.

The son immediately set out to live the life of which he had always dreamed. Fine food, wild parties, lots of girls, and lots of friends. The fun lasted until the money ran out. Then things got worse. A famine hit the land and food and work were scarce. The young son struggled to survive and only did so by finding a job feeding pigs and sharing their food. His situation was the definition of rock bottom.

The young son then had a hope-filled idea. The servants in his father's house were in a much better situation than he was. What if he could go back and be his father's servant? And off he went.

While he was still a long way off, the father saw the young son coming up the road and he ran out to him. Hugging and kissing his son, he shouted to his servants to bring some clean clothes and get a meal prepared because they were going to have a party. His son who was dead is now alive! (adapted from Luke 15:11–24)

We are all that son. God is the father who forgives our rebellion and welcomes us back.

Okay, you might be thinking, when that person who hurt me finally realizes he was wrong, like the son in the story, I will forgive them and show love.

God loves us better than that. You see, God didn't wait for us to ask for forgiveness before he paid for it: "But God showed his great love for us by sending Christ to die for us while we were still sinners" (Romans 5:8).

While we were *still* sinners. Before we turned to him. Before we realized our error. God loved us before all of that, while we were still sinners. He loved us while we were still his enemies.

God's desire is for us to reflect his character. When it comes to forgiveness and love, he set the example for us to follow. In fact, unless we can get our minds wrapped around the idea of loving our enemies and forgiving them, then we really won't be able to get our minds wrapped around God's forgiveness and love for us.

Are you familiar with the Lord's Prayer? There is a line in it on this topic: "and forgive us our sins, as we have forgiven those who sin against us." God's forgiveness to us is connected to our forgiveness of others.

Just look at what Jesus tells his disciples immediately following the Lord's Prayer. Jesus said, "If you forgive those who sin against you, your heavenly Father will forgive you. But if you refuse to forgive others, your Father will not forgive your sins" (Matthew 6:14–15).

Forgiven people forgive people.

The barrier to forgiveness is anger. The anger we are feeling is real. The anger is often justified. Sometimes the anger feels kind of good. But the problem is that over time it eats you up inside.

Anger is a powerful emotion. Left unchecked, it has led to some of the darkest moments in human history.

In 1994, in the small African nation of Rwanda, ethnic conflict and anger escalated to genocide. Within one hundred days nearly one million people were murdered. That is 10% of the entire population. The violence was severe. This was not warfare with machine guns and bombs killing people at a distance. The majority of the victims died by the blades of machetes at the hands of their neighbors and fellow villagers.

Years of anger had been building up between the Hutu and Tutsi tribes, but no one thought it would get this bad.

The violence was eventually ended, and a new government began putting the pieces back together again. The country was decimated. Where do you begin to rebuild?

With a country full of murderers, how do you begin to administer justice?

In a word, forgiveness.

A 2017 article in *The New York Times*, "How a Nation Reconciles After Genocide Killed Nearly a Million People," tracks the progress that Prison Fellowship Rwanda is making in this effort. People who were sentenced to prison for the murders they committed during the genocide have the opportunity to have their sentences reduced by seeking forgiveness. The story follows the account of Mathias Sendegeya and Jacqueline Mukamana. Ms. Mukamana was seventeen years old when Mr. Sendegeya killed her entire family.

Upon release from prison, participants in the program are sent to live in a "reconciliation village" with members of the family that they killed.

They are now raising a new generation of Rwandans. Mr. Sendegeya has a wife and nine children — six who were born before he went to prison and three who were born after he came back.

Ms. Mukamana and her husband have four children. She has taught them about the history of the genocide, and she said that they knew the role that Mr. Sendegeya had played in killing members of their family, but that they had never feared him.

"Our children have no problem among them," Mr. Sendegeya said.

Her children will go to his home to make meals, and she sometimes asks him to look after her children when she is away.

"This is the entrance of my home," Ms. Mukamana said, gesturing to her front door, steps away from where the pair sat together. "Whenever he encounters problems, he may call me and ask for help, and it is the same thing for me."[2]

The power of forgiveness and the beauty of loving your enemy.

Anger limits your ability to connect with others. It creates a wall between you and the world. Unchecked anger brings about division in our lives. When we love our enemies, we overcome anger with forgiveness.

Challenge #5

Show forgiveness to someone who hurt you.

There are obviously varying degrees of forgiveness. You can forgive the friend who forgot your birthday. It was hurtful and unkind, but forgivable. You can also forgive the person who spread rumors about you at work and damaged your reputation. It was a damaging and long-lasting pain that followed you for quite some time, but forgivable. You can also forgive the abuser. They took something away from you that can never be replaced or repaired; the trauma inflicted is a constant reminder of what they did, but it is forgivable.

I do not know what burden you carry from past hurts and pains, but I do know you were not designed to bear that burden. To forgive is not to excuse the person's behavior or

---

2. Megan Specia, "How a Nation Reconciles After Genocide Killed Nearly a Million People," *The New York Times*, April 25, 2017. Accessed online.

pretend that you don't hurt anymore. To forgive is to release the debt that is owed you.

But what if they don't deserve it? They don't, just like we don't deserve God's forgiveness.

But what if they didn't ask for it? Forgiveness is not about them. It is about you releasing the burden and anger you are carrying.

What if they don't even know they hurt me? Once again this is about you, not them. Forgive.

What if they keep doing it? How many times do I have to forgive?

Interesting question. Peter asked Jesus the same thing: "'Lord, how often should I forgive someone who sins against me? Seven times?' 'No, not seven times,' Jesus replied, 'but seventy times seven!'" (Matthew 18:21–22).

I think Peter was being very generous by offering to forgive someone seven times! Most people I ask suggest three. Three strikes and you're out—if it is good enough for baseball, it is good enough for my relationships. In his response, Jesus uses hyperbole. That's fancy talk to mean we are not supposed to keep track until we have forgiven someone exactly 490 times (70 times 7). Jesus is telling us to just keep on forgiving. There is no limit . . . just like there is no limit to his forgiveness. If Jesus only forgave us 490 times I would never have made it out of junior high!

To complete the challenge you need to forgive someone.

This might mean setting up a meeting in person or making a phone call. You could write a letter or send an email. Before doing this, let me give you a few tips I have picked up over the years.

If you are going to send written communication, have someone you trust read it before you send it. When we communicate with someone in person the tone of our voice and the expressions on our face add a lot to the interpretation. When we write a letter or email, we are leaving out some of those important clues that reflect our tone. Therefore written communication can often come across more harshly than we intend. A trusted friend can help you make sure this isn't the case.

Perhaps the trauma you experienced is so severe that you cannot imagine ever facing that person. Or maybe the person who hurt you is no longer alive to have a conversation with. Remember, forgiveness is about you. Write a letter to them that you never send or have a conversation with an empty chair representing them.

There is a man in my small group who took on this challenge with regard to his mother. Their relationship had been strained for many years because of his mother's inattention to him growing up. She had him at a young age and was more concerned with her next relationship than with her son. He was angry at his mom. He couldn't believe how selfish she had been all those years. God placed it on his heart that she was to be the recipient of his forgiveness.

The problem was that she was so self-centered that she didn't even know there was an issue. He did not believe bringing up these issues and "forgiving her" would bring any semblance of peace to their troubled relationship. So, he chose to have a conversation with an empty chair. This grown man with four children of his own pretended that his mother was sitting across from him in that empty chair. He told her how much he was hurt and how angry it had made him over the years. Then he forgave her. He actually spoke the words out loud.

He was so excited to share with the group the next week. Not only had he taken the challenge to forgive, he also did something he hadn't done in years: he sent his mom a Mother's Day card. "He even wrote a nice note in it!" his wife chimed in.

We overcome anger with forgiveness.

Chapter 7

Unity Is the Gift of Love

A Catholic bishop, a Baptist-trained pastor, and a Charismatic preacher have dinner together. This sounds like the start to a good joke, but it is actually a true story.

Depending on your background, you are probably either shocked by a meeting like this or you are wondering what the big deal is. For people outside the Christian community this doesn't seem unusual: a group of Christian leaders got together for dinner. But we Christians are very particular about our distinctions.

Up until the eleventh century there was only one Christian Church. But then came the first division: the east separated itself from the west because of a myriad of issues involving interpretation of Scripture, leadership structures, and corruption. (That is a bit of an over-simplification, but it's enough detail for our purposes here.) This new reality of two churches existed for another four hundred years or so until the Reformation, when there was another split in the Church. Now there was the Eastern Catholic Church, the Western Catholic Church, and a group of protesters against the Catholic Church. The divide was again based on interpretation of Scripture, leadership structures, and corruption. This group of protesters were eventually given a name: Protestants.

Although the Protestants were given a unifying name, there was very little agreement over the years on exactly how the church was supposed to operate. There were more disagreements among the Protestants about Scripture, leadership structures, and, unfortunately, corruption. We now stand here five hundred years later with over thirty thousand different Christian denominations. Each one broke off from another group because of disagreements and the inability or unwillingness to solve the conflicts that arose.

The trend is only growing. Every year new denominations are launched by leaders who believe they have a "distinct calling from God" to leave the group they are in. Individual churches split over disagreements in their congregations. What takes place next looks like a nasty divorce proceeding as the splintering parties divide up the assets. Who gets the building? What about the church van? Who is going to keep the food pantry running? It is a slippery slope once one heads down the path of division.

Division brings more division.

So, if you were wondering why it's a big deal for a Catholic, a Baptist, and a Charismatic to have dinner together, well, now you know.

It was a mutual friend who brought them all together, a local businessman. As the conversation unfolded around the table that night, years of baggage and tension melted away as each man got to know the others personally. There wasn't any talk of religious practices or church doctrine, but they did talk about Jesus. They talked about their love for and devotion to him. They talked about their individual faith journeys and how they came to trust him with their lives. As the conversation wore on that night the divisions that these men had inherited from their denominational roots faded into the background.

As the night grew to a close they knew something significant had happened. A simple "goodbye" or "see you later" was not going to bring this evening to the end it deserved, so they decided to pray together. As they prayed,

God placed the following Scripture on their hearts, and they read it together.

> "I am praying not only for these disciples but also for all who will ever believe in me through their message. I pray that they will all be one, just as you and I are one—as you are in me, Father, and I am in you. And may they be in us so that the world will believe you sent me." (John 17:20–21)

This passage comes from Jesus' last night with his disciples before his death. As the Last Supper was ending, Jesus took the time to pray for his disciples. But he did not pray only for the disciples in the room that night; he prayed for you and me as well. He prayed for "all who will ever believe." How powerful is it that on that final night Jesus prayed for us, and now we are here reading these words almost two thousand years later?

Think about all the things Jesus could have prayed for. I mean, he knew what was going to happen in the next few days, hours, and years.

He could have prayed for believers' courage, faith, success, resilience, safety.

All of these things would have served his followers well that night and in the years to come as they took the gospel message to the ends of the earth.

Instead, Jesus prayed for unity.

Jesus prayed that his followers would be one, just as he and the Father are one. The result of this unity demonstrated among Jesus' followers would be that "the world will believe."

As the three men finished their time of prayer together that evening several years ago, they knew that this was not going to be a one-time event. The prayer of John chapter

17 inspired them to continue meeting and to invite others to participate as well. The word spread and several groups started meeting in the metro Phoenix area. I soon became involved as well. I had been meeting with pastors and leaders from my geographical area for years. It wasn't an intentional act to live out John chapter 17; I had simply been exposed to crossing denominational boundaries early in my ministry with the Purpose Driven Network. But now I found myself having coffee with the local Catholic priest and discovering what we had in common.

The word spread and other fellowships began meeting in New York and Portland. It wasn't really organized. I mean, what is there to organize about talking around a table? But it had a profound impact on those who took the time to meet with someone outside their denominational tribe.

The movement spread by word of mouth. And boy, did it spread—all the way to Rome!

Pope Francis heard about a crazy group of pastors and priests getting together for meals and fellowship and wanted to know what it was all about. So he asked us to come and meet with him.

When I first got the call, I assumed it was a joke. There was no way I was invited to a meeting with the pope. But there I was, several weeks later, on my way to Rome with a group of pastors from Phoenix, Portland, and New York to discuss unity in the Church with Pope Francis.

I had heard about audiences with the pope. We got a briefing on what to expect, the formality and protocol required. I had seen footage on the evening news as the pope received guests and held councils, but none of this prepared me for our encounter.

Pope Francis walked into the room unannounced. No choir, no fanfare—not even a guard was present. All the protocol ran through our minds, but he blew us all away by asking how *we* wanted the meeting to go. We had prepared for many things, but not for that. So, we went to our default. We did what we always did when we got together: we sang a chorus, spent some time in prayer, and had a conversation. For almost three hours we talked about unity in the Church.

The focus was not on solving the differences each group held in doctrine. Theologians have been working on those issues for almost a thousand years. Pope Francis did say that he was confident that all theologians will one day come into complete doctrinal unity . . . the day after Jesus returns. Instead, we had stumbled upon the only possible pathway to unity in the Body of Christ: relational reconciliation.

Since then the John 17 Movement has spread to Europe and South America. It has become a major emphasis of CHARIS, the Catholic Charismatic Renewal International Service. And on occasion Pope Francis will lift it up as an example of how we should pursue unity in the Church. And there is no program to follow. It's all about relationship.

Some people have a hard time believing me when I tell them about relational unity in the Body. I think it's our conspiracy mindset that thinks there is always something more sinister going on underneath the surface. I have been accused of trying to lead our church to become Catholic. I even had a family leave our church because they believed I was trying to create a One World Religion with the "antichrist" himself, Pope Francis.

When our eschatology drives our Christology and ecclesiology we get ourselves into trouble.

Sorry, I had to throw in some big theological words to prove that I did go to seminary.

Eschatology is the study of how everything wraps up here on earth. Death, judgment, and—one of my denomination's favorite topics—"the end times." These are the events prophesied primarily in the Old Testament book of Daniel and the final book of the New Testament, Revelation. There is a lot of interpretation involved in these passages because they are the records of visions shown to Daniel and John. There is a lot of symbolism and there is quite a bit of disagreement over how the visions relate to actual historical events and how the events will play out in the future.

Revelation chapter 13 describes a scary account of a world leader rising to absolute authority over all the earth, creating a single government over all. As time progresses the political leader becomes a spiritual leader too, as everyone is required to worship him. It is all very complicated, as one needs to interpret a lot of imagery and symbolism, so it makes for a very interesting Bible study. Over the years several authors have developed novels in order to give a cohesive storyline to these amazing end times events. They did their research, studied all the texts, and filled in the gaps to make captivating stories for us to read.

The problem is that many Christians walked away from these book series with some very bad theology. No, I am not talking about the order of specific events or the interpretation of the symbolism. I am talking about the big concept many walked away with:

The antichrist made everyone follow him in one government. The antichrist made everyone worship him in one religion. The antichrist is evil. The antichrist forced unity, so unity is evil.

This conclusion formed the basis for people's eschatology (the beliefs about future events), which in turn shapes their Christology (the way they view the person, nature, and role of Jesus), and their ecclesiology (the way they view the nature and structure of the Church).

Doesn't this seem a bit backward? It goes against the direct teaching of Christ: "I pray that they will all be one, just as you and I are one," as well as the basic teachings of the Church.

> There is one Lord, one faith, one baptism,
> one God and Father of all,
> who is over all, in all, and living through all.

(Ephesians 4:5–6)

The pursuit of unity cannot be seen as a negative in the Body of Christ.

Our previous pathways toward unity as Christians, such as debating the doctrinal differences and traditions we all hold dear, have not produced much progress. But in fact, such a debate is not even required for unity, because unity is not uniformity. You do not have to be exactly the same as someone or even agree with everything someone believes to be in unity with them . . . just ask my wife!

Denominations have also pursued working together on specific initiatives, pursuing ministerial and missionary cooperation in the Body of Christ. This has seen some limited success. A few years ago, Greg Laurie came to town to hold an evangelistic crusade. Hundreds of churches, across denominational lines, came together to support this enormous evangelistic effort because we all cared about people in our community who are far from God. And then the crusade ended, and we went back to doing our own things. We had come together around an event, which was a good thing, but it was not unity.

Unity does not come from solving doctrinal issues or organizing a shared project. The unity that Jesus prayed for on the night he was betrayed comes from love.

Love is the pathway to unity.

That's why relational reconciliation works. When I develop a relationship with someone the bond of love that grows between us builds unity.

The entire conversation Jesus had on his final night with his disciples was about loving each other. He showed them what it looks like to love by washing their feet. He issued a new command to love, not as we love ourselves, but as he loves us. He talked about love as the bond between himself and the Father. All this talk of love concluded with his prayer and desire for unity among his followers.

The result of following the command of Jesus is unity. To put it more simply:

Unity is the gift of love

Once we make the connection between unity and love, we see it throughout the teachings of Jesus and the example of the early Church. We are commanded to love, and the result is unity. Saint Paul said:

> We who are strong must be considerate of those who are sensitive about things like this. We must not just please ourselves. We should help others do what is right and build them up in the Lord. For even Christ didn't live to please himself. As the Scriptures say, "The insults of those who insult you, O God, have fallen on me." Such things were written in the Scriptures long ago to teach us. And the Scriptures give us hope and encouragement as we wait patiently for God's promises to be fulfilled.

> May God, who gives this patience and encouragement, help you live in complete harmony with each other, as is fitting for followers of Christ Jesus. Then all of you can join together with one

voice, giving praise and glory to God, the Father
of our Lord Jesus Christ. (Romans 15:1–6)

Be considerate, help others, build them up, have
patience, offer encouragement. It sounds like a lot of practical acts of love. The result is harmony and "one voice": unity.

The early Church became united through the sacrificial
love they showed to one another.

All the believers were united in heart and mind.
And they felt that what they owned was not their
own, so they shared everything they had. The
apostles testified powerfully to the resurrection
of the Lord Jesus, and God's great blessing was
upon them all. (Acts 4:32–33)

The connection between unity and love is unmistakable, and it can be found throughout the entire New
Testament. Once you start to notice it, you begin to see it
on even larger scales.

For example, in First Corinthians chapter 12, Paul
describes how the church is supposed to operate in perfect
unity like the human body. Each part of the body is different; you have hands, feet, eyes, lungs, etc. Each part is
important and works together to form the whole. It is the
same in the Body of Christ: each member has a different
gift, and all are necessary. He then interrupts himself: "But
now let me show you a way of life that is best of all" (verse
31). In other words, let's not get ahead of ourselves here—
there is something you have to understand first. What does
he talk about next? You guessed it! Love. In fact, it is one of
the most famous and practical passages in all Scripture on
what love looks like. If you have ever been to a wedding,
you have most likely heard it read to the bride and groom:
"Love is patient and kind . . ." (13:4). Paul does it again

in Philippians chapters 1 and 2. The subjects of love and unity are connected in Scripture because unity is the fruit of loving others.

The letter Paul wrote to the church at Ephesus while he was imprisoned, which we referenced briefly earlier, makes this point emphatically:

> Therefore I, a prisoner for serving the Lord, beg you to lead a life worthy of your calling, for you have been called by God. Always be humble and gentle. Be patient with each other, making allowance for each other's faults because of your love. Make every effort to keep yourselves united in the Spirit, binding yourselves together with peace. For there is one body and one Spirit, just as you have been called to one glorious hope for the future.
>
> There is one Lord, one faith, one baptism, one God and Father of all, who is over all, in all, and living through all.
>
> (Ephesians 4:1–6)

Love and unity are directly connected. In fact, that is what each challenge has been about. Each one of Jesus' commands to love breaks down a barrier that causes disunity among us.

Challenge #1: Demonstrate love to someone over whom you have influence or authority.

Jesus calls us to love everyone regardless of position. The mindset of privilege or entitlement is a destructive force in relationships. It creates division between yourself and the people under your authority because of pride, and also creates division between yourself and those who are in authority over you because of jealousy. Relational isolation happens when you view people as means to your own joy and fulfillment in life. When we love everyone regardless of position, we are overcoming privilege with service to others.

Challenge #2: Demonstrate sacrificial love toward someone you know.

Jesus commands us to love sacrificially. When Jesus gave us his "new command" to love one another, he replaced the standard to which we were held. What was previously "love your neighbor as yourself" became "love others as I have loved you." Jesus gave us an example of this love by giving up his life for us on the cross.

Loving in this way goes against our natural tendency to be selfish. Selfishness is a barrier to authentic relationships. No relationship can grow when one or more of the parties is self-serving. Loving sacrificially or generously breaks down the barrier of selfishness. When we love sacrificially, we are overcoming selfishness with generosity.

Challenge #3: Demonstrate love to someone different than you.

Jesus calls us to love those different than us. Our biases form strong barriers to unity. When we hold biases against certain groups, we avoid interaction at all costs. We try to pretend that they and their problems do not exist.

There are ethnic, religious, political, economic, and cultural divides in our world; the list is never ending. When we ignore or avoid entire groups of people, we ignore the pain and suffering they experience as well. A simple act of compassion pushes us beyond bias to encounter the person who is suffering. When we love those different than us, we overcome bias with compassion.

Challenge #4: Love someone difficult to love.

Jesus commands us to love the difficult to love. Why are they so difficult to love? It's usually because their problems are very difficult to solve. We don't like to take on tasks that we can't finish. We don't want to step into problems that cannot be solved. We have an intrinsic fear of failure. I can't fix the person suffering from mental illness. I can't make the homeless person self-sufficient in a few weeks. So, I move on to an easier problem and an easier person to love. Over time our fears cause people to be excluded from our communities because their problems are "unmanageable." The divide widens and unity suffers.

The solution isn't to find a way to solve their problems. The solution is to treat them like the image-bearer of God that they are. It is to be present in their suffering. Presence is an act of love.

When we love the difficult to love we overcome fear with presence.

Challenge #5: Show forgiveness to someone who hurt you.

Jesus commands us to love our enemies. We are to love those who have hurt us, betrayed us, mocked us, and ridiculed us. I am sure you can come up with more than a few extra wounds for the list. Anger is the emotion that designates an enemy, and what a powerful emotion it is. Anger causes division. Anger pushes the two sides apart and destroys the opportunity for unity.

The only chance we have to love our enemy is to first deal with the anger. Forgiveness is the key to working through our anger. When we love our enemies we overcome anger with forgiveness.

———————

Anger, fear, bias, selfishness, and privilege are all barriers to unity. When these things show up in our families, communities, churches, and businesses, unity goes out the window. By living out the commands of Jesus to love we specifically counteract the very things that divide us.

I will say it again: Unity is the gift of love.

So . . . is that it? Is unity the endgame, the goal of it all?

Once we all take seriously the commands of Jesus to love others selflessly, sacrificially, and compassionately. Once we extend that love to people who are different than us and who are difficult to love. Once we love our enemies and forgive others as Christ forgave us. Once we do all that . . . then unity is going to develop among believers and we can all just get along among ourselves as Christians until Jesus returns. Right?

Wrong.

The result of unity is evangelism.

If you continue to read Jesus' prayer for unity in the Church, he shows why it is so important to him.

"I am in them and you are in me. May they experience such perfect unity that the world will know that you sent me and that you love them as much as you love me." (John 17:23)

So "that the world will know."

We see this happening at the very birth of the Church. The early followers lived lives of sacrificial love toward one another and those around them. They shared everything they had with one another and sold their possessions to help the needy. They loved recklessly and the bonds of unity grew. The result was not an internally focused way of living. Acts 2:47 states the impact of their way of life: They were "enjoying the goodwill of all the people. And each day the Lord added to their fellowship those who were being saved."

Evangelism is spreading the good news message of the gospel. Sometimes it gets a bad rap because the methods used to communicate it don't seem like the way one would share good news. Other times we try to scare people into a relationship with God or manipulate them somehow. I love this quote from Mother Teresa about her evangelism efforts in the biography by Kathryn Spink.

> One Indian government official once said to her, "Tell the truth, you would like me to become a Christian, you are praying for that?" and she answered him: "When you possess something really good, you wish for your friends to share it with you. I think Christ is the best thing in the world and I would like all to know him and love him as I do."[3]

This is what evangelism is all about. One beggar telling another where to find food.

---

3.   Kathryn Spink, *Mother Teresa: A Complete Authorized Biography*, Harper SanFrancisco, 1997, p. 254.

Love, unity, and evangelism all work together to bring the mission of God to the world.

In the Book of Revelation, God gives us a glimpse of what it will look like in the future when his plan of redemption is fully realized.

After this I saw a vast crowd, too great to count, from every nation and tribe and people and language, standing in front of the throne and before the Lamb. They were clothed in white robes and held palm branches in their hands. And they were shouting with a great roar,

"Salvation comes from our God
who sits on the throne
and from the Lamb!"

(Revelation 7:9–10)

Not everyone will receive God's grace; many have rejected and will continue to reject it. But that is not God's desire. Jesus ends his parable of the good shepherd who goes out looking for one lost sheep with this bold statement: "In the same way, it is not my heavenly Father's will that even one of these little ones should perish" (Matthew 18:14).

God loves everyone and desires a relationship with them.

Several years ago I was invited to a very special meeting. It wasn't because I had done anything special myself. I went because my mentor, the founding pastor of the church I now lead, was invited and he was too sick to attend.

The meeting was called by Pastor Rick Warren. There wasn't a lot of detail, just a time, location, and something about getting the band back together. Before Rick Warren wrote the book *The Purpose Driven Life* and became well known around the world, he wrote another book called *The Purpose Driven Church*. It laid out the biblical principles of a church built on the Great Commission and the Great Commandment. This book was influential in the launch of my church, Palm Valley Church, back in the year 2000, as it was for thousands of others during this time. Then the scale of *The Purpose Driven Life* and the phenomenon it became pushed *The Purpose Driven Church* and all the training and conferences that helped so many pastors to the back burner.

As twenty or so of us sat out on a patio at the Saddleback Church campus, Rick began to share his heart about getting back to helping pastors. It wasn't because he needed more influence or notoriety. It wasn't because he wanted or needed more money. It was all about that passage from Revelation, which he read to all of us in attendance.

After reading it through once, Rick went back and re-read the words, "every nation and tribe and people and language." He paused to let the words sink in. Then he continued to explain that we know of at least three thousand people groups around the world without a single believer in Jesus Christ. If that Scripture is true, he said, we have some work to do. We need to take the gospel to them. That "we" was not a Saddleback Church "we." It was also not a Southern Baptist (the denomination he belongs to) "we." He was saying this to a group of pastors from various backgrounds and denominations. This was a Body of Christ "we." We, the Church, need to reach the unreached.

As he unfolded the rough strategy that he had been testing out in Rwanda, I became inspired. Local churches helping local churches meet the needs of their communities with love. It is a bit ambitious to think that my church could send people across the world to learn a new language and culture and build the trust and relationships needed to communicate the gospel with a group that has never heard the name of Jesus. But what my church could do is equip the churches that are near neighbors to that unreached group. We can show them that a healthy church whose members love each other and are united in mission will meet the needs of their communities in love. This church can then make the small jump to reach these unreached groups who are near to them.

The vision was exciting. The plan was big. It was definitely a God-sized endeavor and he was calling me to take part. This is how we came to adopt the country of Côte d'Ivoire, where we have been working for the past few years. Progress has been faster than we expected. Since we have been there, a pastor training school has been established to send out local missionaries. The first group of Ivorian missionaries were sent to the northern part of the country last year to plant churches in towns adjacent to several unreached people groups. God is doing big things in Côte d'Ivoire!

God is also doing big things in my community.

We don't get to skip over our own backyards when it comes to sharing the hope and love of Jesus Christ with others. Evangelism isn't something we outsource; it is something we live because we are all participants. In fact, we are called to be God's ambassadors wherever we go.

And all of this is a gift from God, who brought us back to himself through Christ. And God has given us this task of reconciling people to him. For God was in Christ, reconciling the world to himself, no longer counting people's sins against them. And he gave us this wonderful message of reconciliation. So we are Christ's ambassadors; God is making his appeal through us. We speak for Christ when we plead, "Come back to God!"

For God made Christ, who never sinned, to be the offering for our sin, so that we could be made right with God through Christ. (2 Corinthians 5:18–21)

An ambassador represents the person or entity who sent them. Our most common understanding of the role is in a diplomatic sense. The United States sends official ambassadors to every nation with which it has diplomatic relationships. The ambassador is there to represent the United States' interests. They don't make decisions on their own about trade deals and treaties; rather they communicate the desires of the United States government. Ambassadors are very important messengers because their words and actions speak for an entire nation.

No pressure—but you are God's ambassador. You are his messenger to the people he has placed in your life and sphere of influence. The way you act and behave has a direct impact on their view of the God you serve. Like I said, no pressure.

Now do you know why Jesus was so insistent about loving others? If God is love, we must love. If we fail to do so we are a very poor reflection of him. And he loves us enough to tell us and show us how:

Love everyone regardless of position.
Love sacrificially.
Love those different than you.
Love the difficult to love.
Love your enemies.

New City Press

New City Press is one of more than 20 publishing houses sponsored by the Focolare, a movement founded by Chiara Lubich to help bring about the realization of Jesus' prayer: "That all may be one" (John 17:21). In view of that goal, New City Press publishes books and resources that enrich the lives of people and help all to strive toward the unity of the entire human family. We are a member of the Association of Catholic Publishers.

www.newcitypress.com
202 Comforter Blvd.
Hyde Park, New York

Periodicals
Living City Magazine
www.livingcitymagazine.com

Scan to join our mailing list
for discounts and promotions
or go to www.newcitypress.com
and click on "join our email list."